THE COLD WAR FALLOUT:
BOUNDARY & CONFLICT
IN THE HORN OF AFRICA

THE COLD WAR FALLOUT: BOUNDARY & CONFLICT IN THE HORN OF AFRICA

Abdisalam M. Issa-Salwe

Looh Press | 2022

LOOH PRESS LTD.
Copyright © Abdisalam M. Issa-Salwe 2022.
Second Edition, First Print August 2022

All rights reserved. No part of this publication may be reproduced, stored in any retrieval system, or transmitted in any form or by any means, including photocopying, recording, or other electronic or mechanical methods, without the prior written permission of the publisher, except in the case of brief quotations embodied in critical reviews and certain other noncommercial uses permitted by copyright law. For permission and requests, write to the publisher, at the address below.

Xuquuqda oo dhan way dhawran tahay. Buuggan oo dhan ama qayb ka mid ah lama daabacan karo, lamana tarjuman karo la'aanta idan qoran oo laga helo qoraha.

First Edition 2001	***Daabacaadda Kowaad 2001***
"The Cold War Fallout: Boundary and Conflict in the Horn of Africa"	"The Cold War Fallout: Boundary and Conflict in the Horn of Africa"
Haan Publishing,	Haan Publishing,
London, UK.	London, Ingiriiska.
Second Edition 2022	***Daabacaadda Labaad 2022***
"The Cold War Fallout: Boundary and Conflict in the Horn of Africa"	"The Cold War Fallout: Boundary and Conflict in the Horn of Africa"
Looh Press Ltd.	Looh Press Ltd.
Leicester, England, UK	Lester, Ingiriirska, UK

Printed & Distributed by
Looh Press
56 Lethbridge Close
Leicester, LE1 2EB,
England, UK
www.LoohPress.com
admin@LoohPress.com

Printed & bounded by: *Waxaa Daabacay:*	TJ Books. Cornwall, England.
ISBN:	978-1-912411-44-3 **(Paperback)**

To my aunt Xaawa-Geni Ismaaciil Boqor.

"Unlike any other border problem in Africa, the entire length of the existing boundaries, as imposed by the colonialists, cut across the traditional pastures of our nomadic population.

The problem becomes unique when it is realised that no other nation in Africa finds itself totally divided along the whole length of its borders from its own people".

Adan Abdulle Osman, President of the Somali Republic, (1960-67).

"The Strategic Arms Limitation Talks (SALT) lies buried in the sands of the Ogaden"

Zbigniew Brzezinski, US National Security Adviser (1978-80).

CONTENTS

ACKNOWLEDGEMENTS xi
PREFACE xiii
NOTES ON TERMINOLOGY xv
INTRODUCTION 1

CHAPTER ONE
THE HISTORICAL CONTEXT 11
   PRE-COLONIAL AFRICA AND THE QUESTION OF
   FRONTIERS 11
   BOUNDARY-MAKING 13
   BOUNDARY CONCERN IN AFRICAN NATIONALISM 15
   PREPARING FOR THE FUTURE 16
   THE PROBLEM OF COLONIAL BOUNDARIES FOR
   INDEPENDENT AFRICA 17
   THE POTENTIAL FOR IRREDENTISM IN AFRICA 20
   OVERVIEW OF IRREDENTIST CLAIMS IN AFRICA 21
   TERRITORIAL COMPROMISE 23

CHAPTER TWO
THE DOCTRINE OF NATIONAL
SELF-DETERMINATION AND AFRICAN UNITY 27

THE PRINCIPLE OF UTI POSSIDETIS AND THE RIGHT OF
SELF-DETERMINATION...27
ON THE ROAD TO UNITY...29
THE OAU: AN ATTEMPT TO ANSWER AFRICA'S PRESSING
ISSUES..31
THE OAU CHARTER AND THE PRINCIPLE OF AFRICAN
UNITY...33
THE SELF-IMAGE OF THE NEWLY INDEPENDENT STATES
OF AFRICA...35
THE CONFLICT BETWEEN THE PRINCIPLE OF UTI
POSSIDETIS AND SELF-DETERMINATION............................38
DEALING WITH DISPUTES...39
REGIONAL LAW VS. INTERNATIONAL LAW......................42

CHAPTER THREE
EAST-WEST STRATEGIC
COMPETITION IN AFRICA...43
THE COLD WAR AND AFRICA...44
THE SOVIET ROLE IN AFRICA...46
SOVIET POLITICAL INFLUENCE...49
THE SOVIET-WESTERN CONFRONTATION IN AFRICA 51

CHAPTER FOUR
THE HISTORICAL CONTEXT OF
THE CONFLICT OF THE HORN..55
POST-WAR OUTCOME...62
THE SOCIO-ECONOMIC FACTOR...67

CHAPTER FIVE
SOMALI NATIONALISM AND
FRONTIER REVISION..71
SOMALIA'S TERRITORIAL CLAIMS.......................................74
ATTEMPTS TO SOLVE THE DISPUTES..................................77
SOMALIA'S DISPUTE WITH ETHIOPIA.................................78
THE BACKGROUND OF THE SOMALI-ETHIOPIAN
BOUNDARY DISPUTE..80
POST-COLONIAL ERA..82
ETHIOPIA'S CLAIMS..84

SOMALI-ETHIOPIAN DIPLOMATIC CONTACT 86
SOMALIA'S DISPUTE WITH KENYA 89
THE NORTHERN FRONTIER DISTRICT ISSUE 91
THE AFTERMATH 94
KENYAN-SOMALI DIPLOMATIC CONTACT 95
SOMALIA'S DISPUTE WITH FRANCE 96
SOMALIA'S DIPLOMATIC TACTICS 101
QUIET DIPLOMACY: THE PROCESS OF DISENGAGEMENT ... 103
THE DISENGAGEMENT AND DETENTE 106
RELATIVE CALM 108
EXTERNAL FACTORS 112
UNSTABLE DETENTE 113

CHAPTER SIX
THE IMPACT OF
THE COLD WAR IN THE HORN 117
THE SUPERPOWERS IN THE HORN OF AFRICA 120
THE HORN CONFLICT: INSTABILITY IN THE ETHIOPIAN POLITICAL ESTABLISHMENT 124
THE ETHIOPIAN-SOMALI WAR 126
INTERNATIONAL DIMENSIONS OF THE HORN CONFLICT. 128
THE SOVIET-CUBAN MILITARY INVOLVEMENT IN THE HORN 130
WESTERN REACTION 135
THE US DILEMMA: REGIONALIST VS GLOBALIST APPROACH 138

CHAPTER SEVEN
THE IMPACT OF THE END OF
THE COLD WAR IN THE HORN 143
THE IMPACT OF SOMALIA'S IRREDENTIST POLICIES 143
THE WITHDRAWAL OF THE SUPERPOWERS FROM THE HORN 147
THE UNRESOLVED BOUNDARY PROBLEMS 149
THE SOMALI-ETHIOPIAN PEACE AGREEMENT 152
THE PRICE OF PEACE 154

- CONCLUSIONS 157
  - SOMALIA: LOSING THE BATTLE 159
- APPENDIX 163
  - APPENDIX I: THE ORGANIZATION OF AFRICAN UNITY CHARTER 163
  - APPENDIX II: PROTOCOL OF THE COMMISSION OF MEDIATION, CONCILIATION AND ARBITRATION 176
  - APPENDIX III: RESOLUTION OF THE ALL AFRICAN PEOPLES CONFERENCE 181
  - APPENDIX IV (A): TREATIES BETWEEN BRITAIN AND SOMALI TRIBES, 1884-85 183
  - APPENDIX IV (B): SUPPLEMENTARY GENERAL TREATY. 185
  - APPENDIX V: AGREEMENT BETWEEN BRITAIN AND THE OGADEN 186
  - APPENDIX VI: TREATY OF PROTECTION BETWEEN FRANCE AND THE CHIEFS OF THE ISSA SOMALIS....187
- MAPS 189
  - AFRICA 190
  - NORTH-EASTERN SULTANATES 191
  - SECESSION OF JUBBALAND 192
  - THE OGADEN (WESTERN SOMALILAND) 193
  - NORTH-EASTERN DISTRICT FRONTIER (NFD) 194
  - ABYSSINIAN EXPANSION FROM 1887 TO 1891 195
  - PARTITION OF EAST AFRICA INTO SPHERES OF INFLUENCE 1890 TO 1891 196
  - PARTITION OF SOMALI TERRITORY BETWEEN 1888-1894 197
  - MODERN ETHIOPIA 198
- BIBLIOGRAPHY 199
- INDEX 205

ACKNOWLEDGEMENTS

I owe my deepest gratitude to Dr Alan Foster whom, as the Head of Political Pathway, University of Greenwich, London, supervised me during my MA studies at the university in 1995. His invaluable guidance made possible my original dissertation "*The Cold War and Boundary Politics in Africa: The Case of Somalia and the Horn of Africa*" into a penetrating thesis. It was his insight advice and vision, which inspired me to extend the dissertation into a book.

I am also indebted to Mohamed Osman Omar. Mohamed, who not only was involved in the editing and polishing of the manuscript, but also in the intellectual debate of the main topic. Similarly, I am indebted to Haile Indalkachow.

I express my sincere thanks also to Abdullahi Dool who allowed me to dip into his library of reference books and maps. I owe him also for his encouragement.

To my wife, Hawa-Deeqa, I owe my deepest gratitude for her patience during the long nights and days of writing this book.

PREFACE

The violent overthrow of General Mohamed Siyad Barre of Somalia in January 1991 sent Somalia spinning out of control. The subsequent crisis resulted in the disintegration of the Somali state and a civil strife which claimed more than three hundred thousand dead and wounded, with roughly four fifths of its population displaced. Nearly one fifth of the population fled to take refuge in the neighbouring countries and other parts of the world. These displaced people and their children have lost their past as well as future.

The Somali plight, which subsequently engulfed the entire Horn of Africa, triggered a wide debate: Could other states meet the fate of Somalia? What example could the Somali case offer to the future solutions of nation-state 'ailments'? How could the Somali crisis affect the regional and global peace? Could examination of the crisis in a regional and global context, help answer some of the many unanswered questions?

When the European colonial powers left Africa, they left behind a complex legacy of utter disorder of land and people. The newly independent African states were confronted with the task of tackling this complex problem. During the struggle for independence, African nationalist leaders viewed critically the international borders inherited by their states. The feeling of anti-colonial nationalism led them to resent all the arbitrary imposition of borders as well as colonial rule. However, on achieving independence the majority of the African states accepted the boundaries determined by colonial rulers. Defining themselves according to the inherited boundaries, the majority of the African states found it necessary to opt for respect of boundaries, and mutual abstinence from irredentism. However, a few states, including Somalia, rejected this conclusion.

Developing outside the main African thinking, Somali nationalism is based on an ethnic-cultural entity embracing all Somalis. As the cohesion of Somali population was much stronger, in the early years of independence in the 1960s, the logical conclusion was that Somalia was less prone to disintegration than the majority of African states. However, this has proved an illusion. The 1990s development made the breakdown of the Somali state an important case study for scholars of political science, history and international relations.

This book attempts to probe into one of the main issues which manifested in the Horn of Africa crisis: The boundary politics of Africa which has shaped (and still affects) African inter-state relations.

NOTES ON TERMINOLOGY

The terms Western Somaliland and the Ogaden are both used in the text in different places and are intended to reflect the same territorial area. The contiguous geographical areas of the Horn, where Somalis are located, are variously referred to as Somalilands — Western Somaliland, British Somaliland, Italian Somaliland, and sometimes using the article (the British Somaliland) — signifying that these are lands where Somalis live.

The name Ogaden is widely used for the Western Somaliland. It, however, does not denote the whole territory which Somalia claims. To separate the region from Somali identity, Ethiopia named the region Ogaden, a name which indicated simply one of the Ethiopian-Somali ethnic peoples. The Ogaden clan is one of the major Somali clans who live in the region (it can also be found mixed in all the main

Somali clans). Administratively, the Ogaden forms part of the Hararghe Province and stretches from Jigjiga, the region's capital, to the Somali border, a territory exclusively inhabited by ethnic Somalis. In this sense, the Ogaden covers roughly two thirds of the territory which Somalia recognises as Western Somaliland. For Somalia, however, Western Somaliland stretches from Awash Valley in the north-west (just 150 miles from Addis Ababa) round the periphery of the Ethiopian highlands to the east until the Somali border, El-Adde in the east and Moyale in the West.

During the colonial period, the Ogaden was one of the three parts which comprised the Somali inhabited region in Ethiopia. The other two parts were Hawd (Haud) and Reserved Area (see map). In 1887, just a few years after the signing of Anglo-Somali treaties of protection, Britain signed a treaty with Ethiopia. That treaty was to bring Jigjiga under Ethiopian rule, while at the same Britain retained it administratively. Britain also retained the Hawd and the Reserved Area (the other two regions which together comprised Western Somaliland). The 1942 and 1944 Anglo-Ethiopian Agreements which terminated British Military Administration (BMA) of the Hawd (Haud) and Reserved Areas made it possible for Ethiopia to gain the Ogaden, Hawd and Reserved Area from November 1954. While Western Somaliland shows a broader picture of the territorial context and gives the territory a Somali essence, the Ogaden presents a limited picture. In spite of the fact that both names have different meanings, in this text I will use both interchangeably as it is appropriate.

INTRODUCTION

Towards the end of 1970s, two traditional rival armies vied fiercely for the control of a savannah land in Africa. In a blitz, one army overran the other. However, before a victory could be claimed by either warring side, suddenly a "Big Brother" brings succour to, what the diplomatic jargon would call, "the would-be-victim". Within a short time, the conflict assumed an international dimension which threatened global stability. World attention focused breathlessly on the outcome of the bloody contest. How could a land inhabited exclusively by nomads and with no modern economy what-so-ever gain so much attention? What was at stake in this part of the world?

By looking at the location and time of the major components of the jigsaw conflict we may be able to identify the elements which made the conflict assume international proportions: The "Big Brother" was the Soviet Union, which was expanding its influence in the Horn of Africa. The period was the Cold

War (following the energy crisis). The place was the Horn of Africa whose strategic location near the oil-rich Middle East was of great value to Eastern and Western blocs. The other components were just the triggers: the Ogaden region which was the disputed land and Ethiopia and Somalia, the warring countries.

In early 1978 the Soviet Union decided to intervene in the Ogaden war to help Ethiopia. This triggered a competition between Moscow and Washington. The gap developed due to these strains was reflected in Carter's speech of 8 June 1978 when he warned that,

"... this is not a matter of our preference, but a simple recognition of facts. The Soviet Union can choose either confrontation or co-operation."[1]

The period coincided with the time when the US and Russia were negotiating the Strategic Arms Limitation Treaty (SALT). On 27 February 1978, President Jimmy Carter's National Security Adviser, Zbigniew Brzezinski declared that "SALT lies buried in the sands of the Ogaden".[2]

What was the root cause of the conflict which marred East-West relations? In a simple word it was a boundary dispute: a dispute between Ethiopia and Somalia which heightened the volatile relationship of the Horn of Africa states and made the Horn an important arena in which Eastern and Western blocs competed. The conflict exposed

---

1 Legum et al, 1979: 12.
2 Brzezinski, 1983: 186.

also the fragility of the OAU's approach to the territorial policy for the post-colonial states. The newly independent African states felt unequal in tackling the disorder of land and people that the colonialists had left behind.

In the early 1960s, it was widely believed that the inherited borders of the new African states would give rise to many bitter conflicts. The predictions that boundary and territorial conflicts would plague Africa after were based on the assumption that the newly formed African states would not accept the boundaries inherited from colonialists. It was feared that tribes and ethnic groups divided as a result of colonialism would seek to unite, to become members of the same state, or to form a state of their own, and that they would therefore challenge the boundaries dividing them.[3] If secession was granted to any group or region, it was feared that such grant could lead to secessionist demand from other groups or regions, thus threatening the integrity of the state. African leaders trembled at the idea that all people who share a culture should live under a single flag. The noted British expert on African geography, R. J. Harrison Church, also emphasised in mid-1950s that

> "the unrealistic boundaries need revision... and some African peoples will not tolerate much longer their division by such lines."[4]

---

3   Tordoff, 1972: vii-viii.
4   *Ibid.*, vii.

The year 1960 is known as the *annus mirabilis* of African independence as the majority of African states came into existence during that year. By the latter half of the 1990s there were fifty, or (if the Saharan Arab Democratic Republic is included), fifty-one independent states. With only a few exceptions, (such as Ethiopia, Egypt and Liberia), they are 'new' states. As they acquired statehood, the new states began to search for new identities as nation-states. They embarked on the task of welding into a nation a variety of peoples, speaking different languages and at different stages of social and political development.

Boundaries may be called the external shell of the state. Therefore, survival of several new African states depended on protecting the shell. By defining themselves according to the inherited colonial boundaries, the majority of African states found that for their own survival they must respect the inherited colonial borders. In many cases, the maintenance of the *status quo* has come to be associated with self-preservation of the state.

In spite of this, almost all-African states have at one time or another been involved in some border dispute. Two states opposed the principle of accepting inherited boundaries. One of these was Somalia. Somalia's territorial claims, and counter-claims of Ethiopia, Kenya and France (Djibouti) have provoked many international problems.

Somalia's aim was to unite all members of the Somali nation within a Somali nation-state. Somalia's claims can be categorised, according to Touval's definition, as "core values". Claims which concern "core values" of self-image focus upon ethnic distinction.[5] For the Somali people the creation of an independent Somali Republic, on 1 July 1960, was only the beginning of their struggle for national unity. The policy of uniting Somalia's remaining relatives under one flag challenged the principle of accepting existing borders. Many African states were vulnerable and suspicious of any challenge to the colonially defined boundaries for fear that the framework of political entities in the continent might be swept away in an anarchy of tribal and other conflicts.[6]

Both sides of the dispute in the Horn had a cases. While the Horn of Africa states saw Somalia's claims as a threat to their survival as states, for Somalia this constituted a dilemma in what Samatar and Laitin called "a nation in search of a state". Since states are defined by their boundaries, the self-image of Kenya, Ethiopia — and those newly independent African states — became associated with their colonial borders. Both cases were antithesis of each other. Their aims could never be reconciled. And the ensuing conflict became o`ne of the longest disputes in the African continent and it made the Horn a rivalry platform for the superpowers.

Situated near the vital tri-junction of the three continents of Africa, Asia and Europe, the Horn is a region of great strategic importance and it is a hotbed of conflicting interests both internal and external. Since the nineteenth century, this part of the world has rarely witnessed peace,

---

5   *Ibid.*, ix-x.
6   Gobban, 1945: 31.

until new boundaries appeared - witnessing the birth of the Eritrean Republic in 1992. Seen in this perspective, peace and stability have been a long way away in this region, and this has had repercussions for international peace. To protect their respective national interests, the rival countries of the Horn has leaned on external help which in turn has created a situation where external powers can interfere.

What was the political and historical context which shaped these events? How did the resulting conflicts affect regional and world peace? Why did the majority of African states opt for the policy of maintaining inherited borders? How did the Organisation of African Unity (OAU) and the resulting regional organisations try to solve the issue of boundaries? How did the involvement of the superpowers affect the conflict?

Concentrating on the relations between the Horn of Africa states, this study attempts to explore the political boundaries of these states and how it affected their relations. In seeking to answer these questions, it examines the political and historical background of the Horn of Africa's rival parties' (Somalia and Ethiopia, Somalia and Kenya) in the wake of the Cold War.

Chapter One analyses the background and setting of boundaries in the post-colonial era and the process of boundary making. During the struggle, African nationalists viewed with alarm the right assumed by the European powers of exchanging or partitioning countries among them without reference to, or regard for, the wishes of the people.[7] They emphasised that boundaries were to conform to ethnic divisions.

In spite of this initial political trend, post-colonial African leaders changed views and instead came to accept the colonially inherited boundaries. Identifying the self-image of the new independence with their colonial borders, the majority of African states found it necessary to opt for respect of boundaries, and mutual abstinence from irredentism.

The doctrine of self-determination seen from a global and regional perspective is the subject of Chapter Two. In both the United Nations and the Organisation of African Unity Charters, the "inalienable right of all people to self-determination and to freedom" is emphasised. In spite of the fact that the pan-African principles of the right of self-determination could have also led to the rejection of colonial borders, most post-independence African leaders' interpretation of the right of self-determination was applicable to what Rupert Emerson calls, "the colonial territory as a whole, within the inherited boundaries".[8] No section of the population, however, was considered to be entitled to this right. This restriction of the right to self-determination contradicted the prevailing anti-colonial ideology. The weakness of the new states compelled them to seek new ways of establishing their legitimacy. This relationship as pre-condition of the majority of African states' survival,

---

7   Touval, 1972: 19.
8   Ibid, 1972: 32.

shaped by the acceptance of the inherited colonial boundaries, lay the ground for the OAU to place great emphasis on the principle of territorial integrity.

How the conflict in Africa — particularly the Horn of Africa — became a rivalry platform amongst the superpowers will be examined in Chapters Three and Four. These two chapters will look at the regional (Horn of Africa) and continental (Africa) context of the East-West strategic interest in Africa. During the Cold War, the Horn of Africa's strategic location near the oil-rich Middle East was of great value to the superpowers. The vulnerability caused by the dispute heightened the volatile relationship of the Horn of Africa states in the 1970s and early 1980s. To further their strategic interests, both the Soviet Union and the United States poured substantial economic and military assistance into this region.

Chapter Five will examine the case of Somali nationalism and revision of frontiers. Somalia's irredentism policy set out to contest OAU policies towards the boundaries. Some territorial disputes reflected deeply rooted values or "core values" related to the "national self". This chapter also looks at Somalia's relationship with its neighbours, and with other countries, e.g. Arab, Western, Eastern and non-aligned countries.

The question of the effect of the Cold War on the Horn will be the subject of Chapter Six. Similarly, the impact of its end is the subject of analysis in Chapter Seven. Geopolitically, the change of relations between superpowers in the 1989-1990 period led to the marginalisation of Africa in world politics. As the competition of the superpowers of the region diminished with the end of the Cold War, the economic assistance injected into the region ceased. Military regimes like those of Ethiopia and Somalia fell victim to the global political change at the end of the Cold War. In fact, neither governments survived the effect of this development. The worse hit was Somalia.

The collapse of the Somali state in the early 1990s triggered a new debate over the question of how and why this came about. Different theories have been put forward one of which identifies the fundamental malaise as the result of the boundary problems which Africa inherited. Somalia's resources, energy and spirit concentrated on the goal of uniting its remaining kinsmen in Kenya, Djibouti and Ethiopia under one flag. This policy effectively isolated it from the pan-African movement. However, Somalis themselves did not see that pan-Somalism, which was the driving force of their foreign policy, contradicted their pan-Africanism. In fact, they regarded it as an application of the wider principle, since it aimed at a legitimate unification of territories which colonial interests had arbitrarily destroyed. Many OAU member-states, however, saw Somalia's position as troublesome and potentially divisive and were not well disposed towards it.

The Somali irredentism on the question of its alienated territories exhausted Somalia economically, politically and socially. This policy resulted also in heightening insecurity in the Horn of Africa, and making enemies of its neighbours,

Ethiopia and Kenya, and many other potential allies. Somalia was seen as a state at war with others.[9]

Beside this external impact, Somalia had a chronic internal problem which it could not solve in a nation framework. The subsequent crisis combined with the internal problems (economic, social and political) had undermined the state's effectiveness.

Viewed from a politico-historical perspective, this theory explores the external impact on Somali society. As a follower of this school of thought, I will attempt to introduce briefly in this section how the collapse of the Somali state is related to the boundary politics of Africa and to the Cold War (and its conclusion).[10]

---

9   Issa-Salwe, 65-7.
10 *Ibid.,*

CHAPTER ONE
THE HISTORICAL CONTEXT

PRE-COLONIAL AFRICA AND THE QUESTION OF FRONTIERS

European contact with Africa began through missionaries, traders and explorers. The Portuguese began to trade on the west coast in the fifteenth century by establishing a number of coastal forts from which they conducted a profitable trade in gold and ivory, and from the seventeenth century in slaves.[11] In the following years they sailed up the east coast where they encountered fierce Arab competition.`

In most of the continent colonies were not established until the last quarter of the nineteenth century. By 1875,

---

11 Tordoff, 1990: 30.

Britain controlled only the areas of Sierra Leone and the Gold Coast and the areas adjacent to Bathurst and Lagos, while French presence did not extend beyond Senegal in West Africa.[12]

King Leopold II of Belgium's ambitious decision to absorb the whole of the Congo basin and the subsequent German annexation of Cameroon, East Africa, Southwest Africa, and Togoland in 1883, precipitated in the following years the distribution of Africa among European powers — Portugal, Britain, Belgium, France, Spain, Italy and Germany.[13] The Berlin Conference of 1884-5 recognised the existence of a 'Congo Free State' and in turn this signalled France and Britain to extend their spheres of influence. As a result, peoples were split between rival European colonialists.

What was the impetus behind colonialism? Brett claims that the colonialists saw themselves as the guardians of a civilisation with a universal message equally applicable to the whole of the underdeveloped world. This narrow paternalistic view neglects the whole concept of the Berlin Conference of 1884-5 and the trade and business enterprises which the colonial powers pushed into their colonies. Another theory has it that colonies were established to prolong the life of moribund European capitalism.[14] The first view can be seen as having 'elitist' tendencies which usually characterise the colonial interlude as a form of enforced modernisation.

---

12 *Ibid.*, 31.`
13 *Ibid.*, 31.
14 *Ibid.*, 32-3.

Projecting colonialism as an historical accident, the latter view fails to explain the complex motives which led to the creation of colonies; the eagerness of European powers to gain access to raw materials needed for their new industries in the wake of industrial revolution.

Another theory which belongs to the anthropological tradition offers a type of structural functional analysis. This theory glorifies the "static and primitive elements in the African society and unduly exaggerates the functional utility of such elements and institutions of the social structure".[15]

In addition to these schools, a new school of national African historiography has emerged. The historians of this group emphasise the non-political aspects of history and focus attention on the social and economic situations as factors of change.[16] They believe that the preoccupation of the African statesmen and leaders can be more satisfactorily explained by this approach. However, it can be fruitful only when the role of the colonial background in shaping the colonial and post-colonial socio-economic institutions and trends is properly understood.

BOUNDARY-MAKING

Generally, the majority of African borders are believed to be arbitrary and artificial in character. This view stems from the idea that since the borders were imposed recently,

---

15 Bhardwaj, 1979: 67.
16 *Ibid*, 68.

African boundaries are not the outcome of the "slow social, economic, and political developments".[17] The critics of African borders usually refers to the way they were drawn. African borders were created by outside powers without taking into account the wishes of the local population, of local circumstances, such as ethnic distribution, economic needs like land and water use, and communication patterns.

According to Touval, the process of boundary making can be put into two categories: (i) boundaries between territories possessed by different European powers. This type of boundary is defined as boundaries established by international agreement; and (ii) unilateral boundaries which were a result of separating territories belonging to the same European power.[18] Unilateral because they were set by the unilateral act of one government.

The European powers and the African societies concluded treaties. European motives were manifold, but their major interest was to stop European rivals from filling the gap and to gain support for their demand for international recognition of territorial claims. Except for rare cases, the African society often had no choice but to accept European power treaties. The allocation of territories and delimitation of borders were always made by Europeans, but in some instances there were some African societies who aided the concerned powers to establish control in a given territory.

---

17 Touval, 1972: 3.
18 Ibid., 4.

BOUNDARY CONCERN IN AFRICAN NATIONALISM

The border issue and the issue of self-determination were echoed in the National Congress held in Accra in March 1920. That was the first sign of African concern over boundary making by foreign intruders. The Congress adopted a number of resolutions mainly concerning self-government, the franchise and other reforms designed to extend the rights of the African population. One of the resolutions read:

"The Conference views with alarm the right assumed by the European powers of exchanging or partitioning countries between them without reference to, or regard for, the wishes of the people".[19]

The Congress emphasised that boundaries were to conform to ethnic divisions. In spite of that, the Congress did not label itself as pan-Africanist, the Congress policy was pan-Africanism and it had greatly influenced the pan-Africanism movement.

The 1945 pan-African Congress held in Manchester, United Kingdom, also devoted some attention to boundary problems. The Congress passed a resolution which was its first formal condemnation of colonial borders. The resolution was about West Africa and condemned the artificial divisions and territorial boundaries created by the Imperial Powers which deliberately tried to obstruct the political unity of the West Africa peoples.[20] The Congress emphasised that peoples and

---

19 *Ibid., 19.*
20 *Ibid., 21.*

territories should not be disposed of arbitrarily and that ethnic groups ought not to be divided by international boundaries.

PREPARING FOR THE FUTURE

Following independence most African states had closer ties, especially in terms of trade relationship, with European states rather than with each other. Former colonial powers remained the principle trading partners with their respective former colonies, now independent. This relationship exercised considerable leverage within the newly independent states. According to President Kwame Nkrumah of Ghana, this was 'neo-colonialism' as the former colonial powers, while granting formal political independence to their former colonies, retained the economic control. The way out from this nightmare, Nkrumah believed, could be a United Africa. This vision coupled with a "strong sense of emotional commitment to unity, based on racial consciousness and the common experience of colonialism" was the road towards the creation of a continental organisation.

In April 1958 Nkrumah convened a conference in Accra which was attended by Liberia, Egypt, Libya, Morocco, Tunisia, Ethiopia, Sudan and the host country, Ghana. The conference formed the Conference of Independent African States (CIAS). In September the conference formed the pan-African Freedom Movement of East and Central Africa (PAFMECA). Again in December 1958, Nkrumah held a more ambitious conference, the All African People's Conference (AAPC), whose goal was to support and co-ordinate the nationalist struggle in Africa.[21] Representatives included political groups and trade unions of both independent and still dependent African countries. The conference adopted among other things a resolution calling for "wholesale boundary revision along lines to be provided by indigenous cultural, linguistic and economic criteria".[22]

In early 1960 more states joined the AAPC, although, their differences over political issues such as the conflict in Congo, the war in Algeria and Morocco's claim to Mauritania, made both AAPC and CIAS redundant.

New regional groupings emerged in the following years, the most important being the Casablanca bloc, the Brazzaville bloc (also known as Malgache) which opposed each other and the Monrovia group, which was an intermediate group.[23] While the Casablanca bloc leaned towards socialism, the Brazzaville bloc sought to assert an African cultural identity. To reconcile the two opposing groups, a dialogue conference was held in Lagos and Monrovia in 1962, but the rift between the two blocs thwarted any meaningful outcome.

THE PROBLEM OF COLONIAL BOUNDARIES FOR INDEPENDENT AFRICA

In the early 1960s, it was widely believed that the inherited borders of the new African states would give rise to many

---

21 *Ibid.,* 239-40.
22 Mayall, 1983: 81-2.
23 *Ibid.,* 240-1.

bitter conflicts. The predictions that boundary and territorial conflict would plague Africa after independence were based on the assumption that "tribes and ethnic groups divided would seek to become united, to become members of the same state, or form a state of their own", and that they would therefore challenge the boundaries dividing them.[24]

Nkrumah warned in 1958 against the danger inherent in the colonial "legacy of irredentism and tribalism".[25] The noted British scholar on Africa, the geographer R. J. Harrison Church, stated in mid-1950s that "the unrealistic boundaries need revision... and some African peoples will not tolerate much longer their division by such lines."[26]

Nationalism as a movements in Europe was based on ethnically homogenous nations, whereas nationalist movement in Africa revolved around the population of given colonial territory (except few countries). As the populations were in most cases ethnically heterogeneous, the struggle was waged in the name of a territorially defined population. Therefore, their goal was usually independence within the existing territorial administration.

The domestic influence over the boundary politics is one of the aspects involved in state formation. Many states advocated the territorial *status quo* and the sanctity of the boundaries imposed by the colonial powers. The ethnic compositions of

---

24 Touval, 1972: vii-viii.
25 *Ibid.*, vii.
26 *Ibid.*, vii.

these states, their political history and their internal politics were the factors which influenced them towards boundary and territorial problems. Boundaries may be linked to the external shell of the state, therefore, for many new African states their survival got linked to protection of the shell. Maintenance of the *status quo* has come to be associated with the self-preservation of the state.[27] If secession is granted to any group or region, it was feared, it would stimulate secessionist demands from other groups or regions, thus threatening the integration of the state. Many African states were vulnerable and suspicious of any challenge to the boundaries defined by colonialists for fear that the framework of political entities in the continent might be swept away in an anarchy of tribal and other conflicts.[28]

Boundaries can be conducive to peace or to conflict. Lord Curzon expressed the view that borders are "the razor's edge on which hang suspended the modern issues of war and peace," and that borders have an "overwhelming influence" in the history of the modern world.[29]

Despite the fact that almost all African states have at one time or another been involved in some border dispute, four states have been opposed to the principle of accepting the inherited boundaries. These were the Somali Republic, Morocco, Ghana, and Togo. Their irredentist policies caused many conflicts with their neighbours which also became an

---

27 *Ibid.*, 30.
28 Gobban, 1945: 31.
29 Touval, 1972:25.

international concern: conflicts between Somalia and Kenya, Somalia and Ethiopia, Morocco and Algeria, Morocco and Mauritania, and between Ghana and Togo.[30]

THE POTENTIAL FOR IRREDENTISM IN AFRICA

Irredentism, which is believed to be an outgrowth of the complexities inherent in the notion of the nation-state, "highlights the importance of people and the land they occupy in the determination of the frontiers of the state".[31] In most instances, the boundaries of existing states do not coincide with those groups who perceive themselves as culturally cohesive units. The quest of ethnic groups for self-determination has given rise to separatist movements whose demands range from autonomy to full independence, as well as to irredentist claims by governments that seek to retrieve ethnic kin and their territories from neighbouring states.[32]

Some writers define irrendentism in biological terms. For example, Ben-Israel has stated that irredentism relies on the atavistic "call of the wild" of modern nationalism. Although not by the same physical means, according to him, it recalls the instinctive urge of humans to define their territory in the same way that animals do. Irredentism, he concludes, brings into play the biological and territorial sources of nationalism, for which it was condemned by the early opponents of the

---

30 Ibid.,:24.
31 Gazan, 1991:1-2
32 *Ibid*, 1.

principle of nationalism, such as Lord Acton in the mid-nineteenth century.[33] For Acton, the principle of nationalism meant a regressive coarsening of the fabric of human society towards rule by biological and tribal relationships, and by materialistic and accidental facts.

Irredentism is perceived as different and distinct from separatism. The term irredentism (derived from the Italian *irredenta* - unredeemed) has come to encompass any political effort to unite ethnically, historically, or geographically related segments of a population in adjacent countries within a common political framework. In the African context, the potential for irredentism is something to be considered as political surgery which partitioned hundreds of ethnic groups during the colonial scramble for Africa.[34] Most groups were divided into many parts. Some of these groups are the Somalis, Bakongo, Ewe, Zande, Fulani, Ngoni, Chewa, Luanda, and Yao. Many of these partitioned communities have preserved a "dominant or active sense of community" based on common language, religion, culture, kinship ties, and political leadership.

OVERVIEW OF IRREDENTIST CLAIMS IN AFRICA

Besides Somalia's irredentist policy, there are other potential irredentists in Africa. Botswana, Lesotho, and Swaziland have strong irredentist claims. In all three states, the "nation" is

---

33 *Ibid.*, 32-33.
34 Neuberger, 1991: 98.

divided between the nation-state and South Africa. The Swazis, Sothos, and Tswanas lived in South Africa either in distinct homelands or in what was called "white South Africa". In the Southern Africa region the first serious irredentist effort was made by Swaziland in early 1980s when it tried to make a "land deal" with South Africa and to incorporate the Swazi homeland with KaNgwane and the Ingwavuma District of Kwazulu.[35]

Another nation-state that has followed an ethnic irredentist policy is the Libyan Arab Republic as it had territorial ambitions towards portions of Tunisia, Mali, Chad and Niger. In 1970s and 1980s, Libya annexed the Aouzou Strip, and sometimes the whole Borku-Enmedi Tibesti region. In 1981 it even tried to annex the whole of Chad.[36]

Irredentist aspirations have also been strong among the Ewe people in the Togo Republic and the Volta Region of Ghana. The Ewe people shares a common myth of descent and a common language, culture, history, and religion. Another case of ethnic irredentism in post-colonial Africa was the Mauritanian effort in the mid-1970s to establish a Greater Mauritania based on the Hassaniya Arabs of Mauritania and the Western Sahara.

Similar irredentist aspirations were voiced by Gabonese Fang, who wished to unite with fellow Fang in Rio Muni (now part of Equatorial Guinea). Other groups include the

---

35 Ibid., 99.
36 Ibid., 99- 100.

Ibos, Yorubas and Hausas — who have intermittently voiced demands for unification with their kin across border (the Ibos in Cameroon and Fenando Poo, the Hausa in Niger, and the Yoruba in Benin).[37]

The Moroccan irredenta and its dream of a Greater Morocco within Morocco's historical boundaries are another illustration of the persistent influence of pre-colonial history, goal, and sentiments. The Moroccan irredenta led to wars with Algeria and to the protracted and bloody conflict in the Western Sahara. Morocco's claim can be defined as historical; it seeks to restore the boundaries of the ancient Almorabid Empire of the eleventh and twelfth centuries. That claim also included the whole of Mauritania, the Western Sahara, portions of Algeria and Mali, the Spanish enclaves of Ceuta and Metilla.[38] In 1970s OAU admitted the Saharan Arab Democratic Republic in its fold. As reaction, Morocco retracted its membership from the OAU. Another instance of North African historical irredentism, in the 1940s and early 1950s, is the Egyptian claim to the Sudan, based on the perceived historical unity of the Nile Valley.

TERRITORIAL COMPROMISE

Not all Africa's territorial disputes have ended in stalemate or in conflict. There are some territorial disputes which ended in compromise. These were the cases between Mauritania and

---

37 *Ibid.*, 100-1.
38 *Ibid.*, 102.

Mali, Ethiopia and Kenya, Tunisia and Algeria, Morocco and Algeria, and Morocco and Mauritania. In many of these cases negotiations led to agreements which ended the territorial disputes. According to Touval two kinds of agreements should be distinguished: agreements which involved territorial compromise and those ratifying the territorial *status quo*.[39] These agreements became possible because of the change of policy of at least one party in the dispute. In the territorial compromise both parties achieved some part of their territorial claims, while the agreements which involved "ratifying the *status quo*", the side yielding on the territorial claim was compensated in some other way.[40]

A dispute between Ethiopia and Kenya ended in territorial compromise. The dispute was on the Gadaduma region, a small strip of land between Ethiopia and Kenya. However, the dispute concentrated on the Gadaduma wells rather than the whole area. The dispute continued for many years and was considered to be a core value dispute as whoever controlled Gadaduma could control the nomadic tribes of the area. The dispute began in early 1902 when Britain and Ethiopia failed in many instances to agree on the demarcation of this area. The problem continued to mar British-Ethiopian relations, until the end of 1957 when the Anglo-Ethiopian Boundary Commission finalised its report on the issue. However, the Ethiopian government refused to ratify the treaty.[41]

---

39 Touval, 1972: 246.
40 *Ibid.*, 246.
41 Farah, 1993: 81.

The British administration cared for the interests of this region much more than Kenya's post-colonial leaders. In fact, the post-independence Kenyan authorities who were more concerned with the threat Somalia posed to the Kenyan state, conceded to Ethiopia — with a face saving formula — the ownership of Gadaduma wells, while Ethiopia recognised Kenya's possession of the Godama wells.[42] The preamble of the treaty, known as the Treaty of 1970, declared that

> Animated by their ardent desire to draw closer, through good neighbourly relations and perfect harmony, the bonds of brotherly friendships which happily exist between their countries; their countries' ideal for peace and security of the African continent as constituting the solid, unalterable proud foundation of their common policy, wishing to offer to the brotherly peoples of Africa a stimulating example in the application to the fundamental principles of fraternity, as laid down in the Charter of the Organization of African Unity, have resolved and agreed to conclude a Treaty determining the boundary between their two countries and regulating certain matters.[43]

In the same negotiation venue, Kenya and Ethiopia discussed and agreed to create a military alliance. Kenya

---

42 Touval, 1972: 247-8.
43 Farah, 1993: 81.

leaders were set to remove any disagreement which could hinder or mar its future alliance with Ethiopia.

In reaction to the Ethiopian-Kenyan alliance, Somalia protested that such alliance could upset the balance of power in Africa and constitute a "threat to the concept of African Unity".[44]

---

44 Touval, 222.

Chapter Two

THE DOCTRINE OF NATIONAL SELF-DETERMINATION AND AFRICAN UNITY

THE PRINCIPLE OF *UTI POSSIDETIS* AND THE RIGHT OF SELF-DETERMINATION

Self-determination, the notion that people should themselves decide upon their community and its power structure, is the basic principle of political legitimacy in the twentieth century. Historically, the concept of national self-determination was developed in the context of Western liberal thought, and entails the notion of government by consent. Although the principle of self-determination may be in tune with the notion of egalitarian world order, it is ambiguous as a general principle.

Elevated by the United Nations, the concept became the central legitimising principle of contemporary international society. Both the International Covenant on Civil and Political Rights and the International Covenant on Economic, Social and Cultural Rights affirm the right of self-determination. Both declare that,

All peoples have the right of self-determination. By virtue of that right they freely determine their political status and freely pursue their economic, social and cultural development.[45]

The declaration on the Granting of Independence to Colonial Countries and Peoples (Resolution 1514 - XV) which the General Assembly adopted unanimously in 1960 is the most authoritative expression of the right of self-determination. The declaration undertakes a more functional approach which places emphasis upon the fact of subjugation by a racially or ethnically distinct group.

Obviously, the principle of self-determination sometimes challenges existing state structures, the maintenance of whose stability is another goal of the international legal system. This reconciliation effort is emphasised in the UN Charter and almost all UN Resolutions have noted international policy on matters of self-determination. In spite of the fact that the two policies were meant not to reconcile, which policy should prevail was provided by the International Court of Justice (ICJ) in the context of Western Sahara case. Counterposing the policies of self-determination, the case

---

45 Reisman, 1983: 161.

threatened the territorial integrity of an existing state. Both Morocco and Mauritania claimed the territory. The ICJ concluded that the contemporary will of the people, Western Sahara People (known also as Sahrawi), was paramount over past legal claims.[46]

ON THE ROAD TO UNITY

The quest for African unity is rooted in history. It emanated from pan-Africanism which has its origins in nineteenth-century America where the American Colonisation Society for the Establishment of Free Men of Colour of the United States was formed in 1816 in response to the alienation and exploitation of the Negroes with the purpose of repatriating free slaves.[47] The pan-African movement, which gathered momentum at the turn of the twentieth century, fought for the end of the colonial system in Africa and called for the dismantling of the colonial boundaries agreed upon at the Congress of Berlin in 1885, and the creation of a united Africa. The independence of Ghana on 6 March 1957 marked the beginning of a new dawn in Africa.[48]

However, the quest for African unity did not have smooth sailing. The rapidly increasing number of independent African states from 1960 onwards soon brought divisions, based on ideological grounds, in the pan-African movement. Groups

---

46   *Ibid.*, 163.
47   Naldi, 1989: 3.
48   *Ibid.*, 3.

such as the moderate Brazzaville group and the radical Casablanca group were established. The former represented a gradualist approach to African unity and advocated a loose association of states. Led by President Nkrumah, the Casablanca group urged a political union and the creation of a United States of Africa along federal lines under a High Command. A third group composed of seven states, not in the Casablanca group, formed the Monrovia group. This group rejected political integration, but stressed the principles of the sovereignty of states and non-interference in their internal affairs. It also sought unity of aspiration and of action based on African social solidarity and political identity, and particularly urged co-operation in the economic, scientific and technical fields.

By emphasising pan-African solidarity rather than territorial identity, the rhetoric of African nationalism was to assume identity of all Africans in the face of colonial and racial dominance.[49] The main intellectual authority of this trend was Kwame Nkrumah of Ghana. Nkrumah sets his vision on two fronts: the first concerns the boundaries which were drawn by the colonial powers. The second questioned the new African states' ability to get economic independence following independence. According to Nkrumah former colonial powers, while granting formal political independence to their former colonies, would try to retain the control over economies. Nkrumah's solution was the creation of a continental state. The proposal did not get sympathy from

---

49 *Ibid.*, 80-1.

African leaders since it required all African states to come under one political institution.

THE OAU: AN ATTEMPT TO ANSWER AFRICA'S PRESSING ISSUES

In the pursuit for a viable continental organisation representatives of thirty independent African states met in Addis Ababa in May 1963. The conference decided to adopt the constitution of a new international body, the Organisation of African Unity (OAU). Tordoff holds that the determination of African leaders to avoid past failures and the concern of some African leaders that the divisions of Africa's rival groups might be exploited by outside powers were the impetus which made for the success of the Addis Ababa conference.[50] Although the OAU Charter fell short of Nkrumah's vision of African unity, it was a compromise document which accommodated the divergent interests of various groups. The Monrovia group's vision of African unity, based on close co-operation in a number of fields among sovereign states, prevailed.

Four principal institutions were set up, one of which was a commission of mediation, conciliation and arbitration. Composed of twenty-one members, the commission was to settle disputes between member states.

The OAU Charter consists of a preamble, an operative section of thirty-two articles and a protocol. The preamble

---

50 *Ibid.*, 241-2.

lists some of the general objectives and beliefs of the OAU. The most significant tenets are (i) its commitment to the inalienable right of all people to self-determination and to freedom, equality, justice and dignity, (ii) the desire and need to promote greater understanding among their people and co-operation among their respective states; and (iii) the establishment and maintenance of international peace and security, based particularly on the UN Charter.[51]

The Charter lays emphasis on the promotion of unity and solidarity of Africa. Despite the fact that the integrationists were defeated in Addis Ababa, the quest for eventual unity was not abandoned. In fact, unity is interrelated to the defence of sovereignty, independence and territorial integrity. Behind this principle is the affirmation of the principle of *uti possidetis*, or the acceptance of inherited colonial frontiers, and the rejection of the irredentist claims of other African states.[52] This principle encompassed the acceptance of territorial integrity.

Incorporating the principles of sovereignty and territorial integrity, *Article 3* of the Charter called for respect for the territorial sovereignty of member states, and *Article 4* required non-interference in the internal affairs of member states.[53]

The preamble also records the adherence of Member States to the principles enshrined in the UN Charter. With this

---

51 Naldi, 1989: 5.
52 *Ibid.*, 5.
53 *Ibid.*, 151; Samatar, 1987: 138.

OAU's rules are compatible with the UN and its adherence to general international law and human rights.

THE OAU CHARTER AND THE PRINCIPLE OF AFRICAN UNITY

The principles of the OAU were emphasised in *Article 3*, according to which the Member States should adhere to the following tenets:

1. The sovereign equality of all Member States;
2. Non-interference in the internal affairs of States,
3. Respect for the sovereignty and territorial integrity of each state and for its inalienable right to independent existence;
4. Peaceful settlement of disputes by negotiation, mediation, conciliation, or arbitration;
5. Absolute dedication to the total emancipation of the African territories which are still dependent.

The issue of sovereign equality of all Member States *(Paragraph 1)* reflects *Article 2(1)* of the UN Charter; it is also a general principle of international law, and refers to equality in law. However, it is the second principle, that of non-interference in the internal affairs of States, which reflects in part the domestic jurisdiction clause contained in *Article 2(7) of the UN* Charter. It lays emphasis on independence and equality of States, and the right of self-- determination. While *Article 1(2)* calls on member states to develop friendly relation 'based on respect for the principle of equal rights and self-determination of peoples', it is *Article 2(7)* which forbids intervention 'in matters which are essentially within the domestic jurisdiction of any state'.[54]

The African leaders' meeting in Addis Ababa questioned whether they should adopt the principle of endorsing the permanence of inherited colonial frontiers or ignore the question entirely. The outcome was: Respect for the sovereignty and territorial integrity of each state *(paragraph 3)*.

During the independence struggle, African nationalists condemned the frontiers drawn by colonialists. The acceptance of the principle of *uti possidetis* may be attributed to the influence of the pan-African movement. However, this decision did not appease Morocco's and Somalia's outstanding claims to neighbouring territories. Pan-Africanism of both countries is considered weaker than the ideology with which the irredentist sentiment had initially been associated.

Nevertheless, it was the April 1964 OAU meeting in Cairo which clinched this issue. The summit adopted the Resolution on the Intangibility of Frontiers according to which Member States pledged to respect the frontiers existing on their achievement of national independence.[55] The resolution underlined the strong determination against boundary revision and provided a powerful support for the territorial *status quo*.

Somalia objected the resolution, and claimed instead that it must be seen differently. It insisted that its claim against

---

54 *Ibid.* 7.
55 *Ibid.*, 9.

Ethiopia is not bound by the Cairo resolution because the boundaries between them were in dispute at the time of the colonial succession.[56]

THE SELF-IMAGE OF THE NEWLY INDEPENDENT STATES OF AFRICA

As states can be defined by their boundaries, the self-image of the newly independent became associated with their colonial borders. However, commitment to the *status quo* was inconsistent with the current anti-colonial nationalist ideology in Africa. During the struggle for independence nationalist leaders viewed critically the international borders inherited by their states. The feeling of anti-colonial nationalism led them to resent all the arbitrary imposition of borders as well as colonial rule.

Although the right of self-determination for 'all people' has been established as the fundamental ordering principle of contemporary international relations and law, the doctrine has an evocative and provocative force. With the achievement of independence, the principle of self-determination which was formerly voiced by African nationalists has been replaced with the principle of the inviolability of Africa's frontiers.[57] As African nationalist movement revolved around the population of given colonial territory, its goal was usually independence within the existing territorial administration.

---

56 Mayall, 1983: 77.
57 Lewis, 1980: vi.

The OAU claimed to support the self-determination of all African peoples, but in practice it was "committed to protect the existing state order". The reason for the OAU to adopt this restrictive definition, according to James Mayall, involved two sets of considerations. The first was based on the emergence in the contemporary international order of national self-determination as the principle of international legitimacy in general. The second involved the process by which pan-African ideology was 'domesticated' in African diplomacy after 1960.[58] Adapting pan-African ideology to the new political tune, the question of self-determination was to be interpreted only "external" self-determination and only for people subject to colonial or racist rule (e.g. South Africa during the Apartheid rule). On the other hand, it established territorial integrity and non-interference as the governing principle of African inter-state relations. The reason that brought African leaders to 'domesticate' pan-African ideology was fear and insecurity for their newly acquired independence.

The rhetoric of anti-colonial thought had two versions of boundary issues. One version was reflected in the resolutions of the All-African People's Conference (AAPC) held in December 1958.[59] The conference had adopted resolutions calling for "wholesale boundary revision along lines to be provided by indigenous cultural, linguistic and economic

---

58 Mayall, 1983: 77-8.
59 *Ibid.*, 81-2, Tordoff, 1990: 239-40.

criteria".[60] The 1945 pan-African Congress, held in Manchester, also devoted some attention to boundary problems.

Since political leaders in Africa used the language of pan-African solidarity, it became necessary for them to 'domesticate' the concept of pan-African unity "by giving it an official and static interpretation".[61] African unity was now defined in 'static' rather than dynamic terms as self-determination was made synonymous with independence from European colonial rule and the achievement of statehood. African interpretation of the right of self-determination was most applicable to, as Rupert Emerson puts it, "... the colonial territory as a whole, within the inherited boundaries". He further reiterates that "No section of the population, however, defined, was considered entitled to this right".[62] This restriction of the right to self-determination contradicted the prevailing anti-colonial ideology.

The weakness of the new African states compelled them to seek new ways to establish their legitimacy. By defining themselves according to the inherited colonial boundaries, the majority of the African states found that for their own survival they were to respect the *status quo*. Since most states were vulnerable to both internal and external acts of secession, they found it necessary to opt for respect of boundaries, and mutual abstinence from irredentism.[63]

---

60 Mayall, 1983: 81-2.
61 Ibid., 82.
62 Touval, 1972: 32.
63 Ibid.,33.

THE CONFLICT BETWEEN THE PRINCIPLE OF *UTI POSSIDETIS* AND SELF-DETERMINATION

In 1960 a dispute between the north-west African states of Burkina Faso (formerly Upper Volta) and Mali was considered by the ICJ. Both parties requested the ICJ to take account of the principle of the intangibility of frontiers inherited from colonial times in determining their common frontiers. However, in its judgement, the ICJ considered it necessary to emphasise the principle of *uti possidetis*, declaring that it had become one of universal application. According to Naldi, ICJ's conclusion would have appeared acceptable if it had been able to establish that the principle of *uti possidetis* was a customary rule of international law at the time. However, he reiterates that although the practice may not be irrelevant to the case, "the ICJ took little account of the rule of intertemporal law which requires that the situation be determined by the rule of international laws as they existed at that time, and not the standards of today".[64]

Nevertheless, the ICJ hinted that there was an apparent conflict between the principle of *uti possidetis* and self-determination. However, African states' decision to adopt and maintain the territorial *status quo* silenced the matter. Despite the fact that the ICJ suggested that the right to self-determination is qualified in Africa, it did not elaborate further to clarify the relationship between the two principles which has long been a source of controversy.

---

64 *Ibid.*, 10.

DEALING WITH DISPUTES

As the continent was riven with disputes, African leaders remained committed to the principle of peaceful settlement of disputes. Where dispute arises, *Paragraph 4 is* adaptable, as it provides for peaceful settlement of disputes by negotiation, mediation, conciliation or arbitration and its analogues to *Article 2(2)* and *Article 33, paragraph 1* of the UN Charter. *Paragraph 4 is* further supplemented by *Article 19*, which establishes a Commission of Mediation, Conciliation and Arbitration, and the Protocol on the Commission of Mediation, Conciliation and Arbitration.[65] The commitment to the principle of peaceful settlement of disputes was perceived to be an indispensable condition to the development of Africa. Member States had pledged themselves to settle disputes peacefully. Under international law States are urged to refrain from the use of threat of force in settling their disputes.

Paragraph 6 urges the member states and the OAU to commit themselves to the total emancipation of dependent African territories and complements the undertaking in the preamble to fight neo-colonialism in all forms. This task was given to the OAU's Liberation Committee. The committee was charged with co-ordinating aid to liberation movements in the continent. *Paragraph 6* emphasised the right of self-determination as a norm of international law applicable to the decolonisation of non-self-governing territories according to

---

65 *Ibid.*, 10-1.

which "their inhabitants can freely determine their political status".[66]

Nevertheless, African leaders did not miss the opportunity to seal this controversial matter. They adopted the Banjul Charter which declares that the right to self-determination does not encompass a right to secession.[67] The Banjul Charter is one of the few international conventions that proclaims self-determination as a fundamental human right. It attempts to address some of the thorny issues about self-determination. Its *Article 20*, (all peoples shall have the right to existence) enshrines the inalienable right to political and economic self- determination.

Paragraph 1 of this article declares that all people have the right to existence and the right to self-determination. This question is further stressed in *paragraph 2* which includes not only national communities but also colonised and oppressed people "who have the right to free themselves from the bonds of domination by resorting to any means recognised by the international community".[68] By establishing that the inhabitants of non self-governing territories have the right to decide about their political, economic and cultural freedom, the self-determination context is synonymous with independence.

---

66 *Ibid.*, 11.
67 *Ibid.*, 10.
68 *Ibid.*, 125-6.

However, when the exercise of the right involves a threat of secession the matter is viewed differently. The emphasis on the principle of the territorial integrity and *uti possidetis* by the African states was meant to avoid this happening. Self-determination does not operate 'internally' as once independence is attained the right to self-determination ceases. However, this right does not extend to those whose rights are being violated by a tyrannical ruler or are persecuted because of ethnic descent. *Paragraph 6 of the General Assembly Resolution 1514*

(XV) Declaration on the Granting of Independence to Colonial Countries and Peoples 1960, reinforces member states authority to reject a right to self-determination which violates the integrity of another state.[69] Any involvement of a state would be taken as violation of the internal affairs of that state.

What means can a given oppressed people adopt to liberate themselves? There seems to be general agreement that political and non-violent opposition is permissible. While the Western states claim that the use of force is permissible if prior force is used by the occupying power, the Third World held the view that the use of force is valid because the "forcible deprivation of a people's right to self-determination is a violation of international law".[70] The deprivation of self-determination occurs where force is already used. Therefore, a self-determination unit has the right to self-defence.

---

69 *Ibid.*, 126.
70 *Ibid.*, 126-7.

REGIONAL LAW VS. INTERNATIONAL LAW

Commonly, where a regional law clashes with an international law, the latter supersedes the former. When the issue is a fundamental policy of the UN the matter is supposed to have heavier weight. However, this does not apply to OAU's resolution of 1964 on boundaries (AHG/Res 171). The border issue was first mentioned in the National Congress held in Accra in March 1920. One of the resolutions viewed with alarm the right assumed by the European powers of exchanging or partitioning countries among them without reference to, or regard for, the wishes of the people. The 1945 pan-African Congress held in Manchester also devoted attention to boundary problems. The Congress passed a resolution which was the first formal condemnation of colonial borders thus emphasising that peoples and territories should not be disposed of arbitrarily and that ethnic groups ought not to be divided.[71]

The idea behind this principle was self-determination. While the OAU Charter expresses concern for principle of territorial integrity, it affirms 'the inalienable right of all people to control their own destiny'. This principle was incorporated from the United Nations Charter.

---

71 Touval, 1972: 19.

Chapter Three
EAST-WEST STRATEGIC COMPETITION IN AFRICA

The main element of the Cold War between the two post-war superpowers lay in the mutual hostility and fear of the antagonist. This animosity had its roots in their several historical and political differences as they were strongly stimulated by the myths which at times turned hostility into hatred. In the eyes of Soviet Union the West was inspired by capitalist values which called for the destruction of the Soviet Union and the annihilation of communism by any means available but, above all, by force or the threat of irresistible force. In western eyes the Soviet Union was dedicated to establishing hegemony of Soviet state and communism over the world and was capable of achieving, or at least initiating, this destructive and evil course by armed forces abetted by subversion.[72] Lack of understanding of each others' historical and political backgrounds led to dramatic manifestations of these prejudices.

The acceleration of hostility was fuelled by growing tension between West and East in the early years which followed the Second Word War. The Cold War protagonists sought to extend their sphere of influence first in Europe then throughout the world.

THE COLD WAR AND AFRICA

In modern history, the African continent has been the object of bitter international rivalry. Britain, France, Spain, Portugal, Germany and Italy have all competed and often fought for possession of various parts of Africa. As colonies became independent, the mode of competition changed to influencing countries indirectly rather than establishing direct control as was the case in the colonial era.[73] Alliances, close co-operation, and peaceful coexistence were the new labels for what are often very one-sided political and economic relationships.

Africa became an important arena of political and ideological conflict for the main actors — the Eastern and Western blocs. One side's gain was seen by the other as its loss. Both the Communist camp and the Western community had vested interest in the future political and economic shape of

---

72 Calvocoressi, 1991: 3.
73 Issa-Salwe, 1996: 78-95.

Africa. The competition was more intense during the Cold War, for the struggle between the two blocs involved not only their power relationships, but what Brzezinski calls, the "clash between two images of the world".[74] The new circumstances and balance of power forced the competing powers to stop short of open aggression. This complex pattern converted the conflict into competition in ideas and the use of other political means such as economic aid.

The Communist impact on Africa had been strengthened by the influence of China which presented itself as a former fellow victim of colonial oppression and exploitation. In spite of the fact that in the early years the Soviet Union and China closely co-operated in establishing links with African nationalism, there were differences between political approaches and aims of Soviet Union and China. This became evident in the early 1959 when a major rift developed between the general foreign policies of Moscow and Beijing which, in turn, affected their respective Africa policies.[75] The vital difference turned on the risks to be taken by both countries in pursuing their common antagonism to the West, and above all to their long-term view on the pattern of Communist political activities.[76]

---

74 Brzezinski, 1964: 3.
75 Lowenthal, 1964: 142-169.
76 *Ibid.*, 184.

THE SOVIET ROLE IN AFRICA

Stalin's death and the subsequent destalinsation of Soviet Russia led to changes in the foreign policy of USSR. One of these policies was a "new outlook and approach towards the developing nations". Soviet policy-makers saw opportunity for political gains in the process of decolonisation. Following this new outlook, they undertook several initiatives aimed at developing relationship with the developing nations many of which were struggling for independence. The new political trend was the culmination of Lenin's vision of forging a union between the nationalist aspirations of the developing world and the revolutionary anti-Western objectives of the Soviet regime".[77]

In spite of pre-Soviet Russia being a major imperial player in Asia in the nineteenth century, one of the major assets of Soviet Union in its appeal to Africa was that it was never part of Africa's colonial past. This distinct asset facilitated its identification with the peoples of Africa struggling against the colonial powers. Its own experience also provided a model for rapid modernisation and economic development.

However, some Sovietologists believe that the Soviet strategy for Africa was based on the Bolshevik distinction between maximum and minimum objectives. They viewed the control of the African continent, with its manpower and resources as the maximum objectives, while the minimum objectives of the communists was to deny Africa to the West,

---

77 Porter, 1984: 16.

and especially to deprive the United States and its allies of political influence, economic opportunity, and strategic bases in Africa.[78]

In the short run, Moscow had seen its best hope in the emergence of African states that would pursue "positive neutrality" and increasingly cultivate close economic, political, and cultural ties with the Soviet bloc. This modest program was later supplemented by more militant aim: to prevent the consolidation of Africa into a separate and solidly non-communist block. At the same time, Moscow began to seek to bank on those states that cast a sympathetic eye on the USSR as a model for modernisation and rapid development, and choosing to concentrate its support selectively on "progressive" states most likely to follow a policy congenial to the USSR.[79]

The general line of the Soviet political strategists since 1955 had been to support African nationalist movements. This aimed at presenting the 'socialist camp' as the champion of anti-colonialism, African independence, and peace and progress. Alexander Dallin has stated that the general strategy of the Soviet Union had been based on three main assumptions. First, to co-operate with existing African governments as there was no reliable African Communist parties. Second, they expected that the growth of trade-union forces, the extension of "front" organisations, and continuing urbanisation and industrialisation would strengthen pro-Soviet elements within African governments. Third, that the Soviet failure to support

---

78 Dallin, 1964: 12-3.
79 Ibid., 13.

and woo the nationalist governments would in effect abandon them to influences and blocs inimical to the USSR.[80]

The Soviet prescription for an "independent" foreign policy for African states begins with the assertion that the "imperialist" powers remained in substantial control of Africa. As the major thrust had been to separate the new African states from the West, the whole arsenal of anti- imperialist propaganda, diplomacy and the measure of Soviet aid had been mobilised to this goal. And to assure its alliance with its new African friends, the Soviet Union also assured them that it would "paralyse" the aggressive intentions of the Western colonisers. By offering the "socialist camp" as a reliable shield for the new nations against the West, Moscow suggested that reliance on the Soviet bloc was essential for Africa's future.[81] In domestic policy Moscow tried to convince Africans that whatever the level of their economic development, size and population, the road of socialism was the only true path of progress.

Moscow was convinced that neither Communist nor "front" organisations were strong enough to lead effectively. This reinforced the decision to maximise the influence of the Soviet state on the national governments of Africa. Following this, since 1958 the Soviet specialists had outlined a series of steps whereby the "progressive" elements in a united front, after its conquest of power, increasingly lined up against the imperialists. And in turn this would pave the way for a

---
80 *Ibid.*, 13-14.
81 *Ibid.*, 15.

new national front under "working class leadership".[82] To legitimise support of national-bourgeois regimes, Soviet theorists devised the concepts of a "non-capitalist path" and "national democracy". This theory implied that it was possible for "any pre-capitalist society to skip over the capitalist stage".[83]

The optimists among Soviet theorists insisted, such a "qualitative" leap would be assisted by several factors: (i) the weakness of the national bourgeoisie, both numerically and economically, and the prospect that the working class would grow more rapidly than the bourgeoisie, (ii) the importance of the state sector of the economy in setting the course for a non-capitalist development; and (iii) the survival of communal land-holding in large parts of tropical Africa.[84]

SOVIET POLITICAL INFLUENCE

During the struggle for independence for many African nationalists socialist ideas were in vogue. While they identified the West with their colonial past, the Soviet Union appealed to Africa for not being part of Africa's colonial past. To understand Africa and provide Soviet policy-makers with information, intelligence and advice about Africa, a variety of techniques had been used by the Soviet Union. This effort extended from academic work to diplomatic and propaganda

---

82 Ibid., 17-8.
83 Ibid., 18.
84 Ibid., 18.

activity, from trade to cultural contact, from economy to military contact.

Until about 1959 Moscow saw Africa as an organic part of the "Afro-Asian" mass. It used to give higher priority to other parts of the "emerging" world, while it was giving second best consideration to Africa. A general sense of optimism pervaded Soviet policy, and an expansive identification with the anti-Western "national-liberation movements" ushered in an era of the Communist "soft sell". Only then did Africa come to attract major attention among Soviet policy-makers.[85]

By 1960 the realities of African politics began to vitiate Moscow's stand as Moscow could no longer invoke the myths of Afro-Asian or all-African solidarity. Moscow was confronted with difficult choices. For example, conflicts such as border disputes or interests between states forced Moscow to differentiate policy. The risk and benefits of taking sides in African struggles were simpler to calculate once the earlier alignments yielded to a new block conforming more closely to Cold War pattern and the "two camp" view.[86]

As early as 1950s, there was emerging in Africa, new regional groupings based on ideological grounds. Most important were the Casablanca bloc and the Brazzaville bloc, which opposed each other and the Monrovia group, which was an intermediate group.[87] While the Casablanca bloc leaned

---

85 *Ibid.*, 20.
86 *Ibid.*, 31.
87 *Ibid.*, 240-1.

towards socialism, the Brazzaville bloc sought to assert an African cultural identity. While the Soviet authorities tried not to antagonise African leaders, they evidently felt obliged to stand with the "progressive" Casablanca group.

However, things did not move as Moscow expected. Once independence was achieved, the new African states no longer looked on the USSR as their natural ally. Following this new development, Soviet policy-makers realised that the new states were by no means interested in a total break with the former colonial powers, whose financial, economic, and technical assistance they needed.[88]

THE SOVIET-WESTERN CONFRONTATION IN AFRICA

In the 1950s and 1960s the Soviet Union's involvement in local conflicts was on a modest scale compared to the 1970s. The USSR attempted — by means of diplomacy, military advisers, arms shipments, and occasionally troops

— to influence the course of at least eight localised conflicts during the decade. The hottest spots were the Indo-Pakistani war, Yom Kippur war, the Ogaden war, the Angolan war, the inter-Communist clash in Indochina, People's Democratic Republic of Yemen clash with Northern Yemen, and the civil war in Afghanistan.[89]

---

88 *Ibid.*, 31.
89 Porter, 1984: 1.

The Soviet Union's debut as a major superpower in African conflicts was marked by its involvement in the Angolan civil war. It was also the beginning of direct intervention by Cuban troops in Africa's conflicts. A majority of African states legitimised the Soviet-Cuban military intervention in Angola as it checked South Africa's military invasion in support of Unita. The fluctuation of the West's indifference to the racist South Africa helped growth of Russia's influence in Africa. However, the legitimisation of the external involvement had another implication over the African states as it was an invitation for non-African powers to step in.

Washington faced a political dilemma whether or not to intervene openly in the Angolan conflict. The effect of such psychological trauma as the fall of Saigon, the fear not to be identified as in defence of racist South Africa made United States not to commit itself in the conflicts.[90] The actions of the superpowers in Angola were intimately connected with the central goals of their respective foreign policies; it was inevitable that the conflict expose the fundamental fragility of detente.

Moscow's political aim was to maintain their global strategic and diplomatic momentum that had been gained with the Communist victory in Vietnam. However, in the eyes of Washington, the Soviet-Cuban intervention in Angola was a dangerous power play and an offensive thrust that went beyond the traditional geographical perimeter of Russian

---

90 *Ibid.*, 170.

interests and beyond accepted post-war rules of game".[91] To the Western analysts, Moscow's aim was to have access to Africa's natural resources, including oil, and to deny these to the West..

As the 1970s progressed, United States foreign policy agenda got focused on the problem of Soviet military involvement in the Third World conflicts. The accession of Brezhnev to power in October 1964 marked the beginning of a third stage of Soviet military involvement in the Third World conflicts.

---

91 Porter, 1984: 147.

CHAPTER FOUR

THE HISTORICAL CONTEXT OF THE CONFLICT OF THE HORN

The opening of the Suez Canal in 1869 created a geopolitical situation which increased the competition among the European colonial powers for control of the coast along the Red Sea and the Indian Ocean. Britain settled in Aden in 1839 using it as a supply station for the route to the Far East. It took interest in the Horn because it was the source of fresh meat and vegetables for its Aden garrison. To prevent other European powers from entering its zone of influence, Britain agreed with Turkey to take the role of direct control of the Red Sea coastal area.

In the early 1860s, the Khedive Ismail of Egypt, in the name of the Pasha of Turkey and the Sublime Porte, began to establish his sovereignty over the ports of the Red Sea by appointing an Egyptian governor for the whole coast from Suez to Cape Guardafui. In 1875 the Egyptians took possession of Zeyla, marched inland and occupied Harar (present Ethiopia) where they set up an administration which was to last ten years.

The Khedive claimed dominion over the whole Red Sea area, including the Somali coast, and despatched a naval expedition to the mouth of the Jubba river to link the southern Sudan and the great lakes with East Africa.

Egyptian troops landed at Kismayo but were withdrawn following a protest from Britain, on behalf of the Sultan of Zanzibar, who also claimed this part of the coast. Britain's objection to the Turkish and Egyptian claim was settled with an agreement signed in September 1877 recognising Egyptian jurisdiction over the Somaliland coast.

The successful uprising in the Sudan by the Mahdist Movement in 1885 precipitated an unexpected geopolitical event in the region. To reinforce its presence in the Sudan, Egypt had to withdraw its forces from the Somaliland coast and the route to Harar.

And to stop its European rivals from filling the vacuum left by the Egyptian withdrawal, the British government from 1884 to 1889 concluded agreements with the coastal Somali clans. On 1 September 1896, a treaty of Protection with the Ogaden people was signed (Appendix). In 1886, Britain and Germany, who were both competing for spheres of influence' in East Africa, agreed to recognise the sovereignty of the Sultan of Zanzibar over parts of the East African coast up to a depth of ten miles, including certain ports as far as Warsheikh. The vagueness of the 1886 Anglo-German Agreement gave Germany a chance to secure possession of the great lakes, for not only was the country north of the River Tana left free to German enterprise, so was the country to the north-west of the British sphere. The matter was settled in 1890 when Germany, in consideration for Britain's secession of Heligoland, withdrew its protectorate over the adjoining coast up to Kismaayo, and surrendered its claims to territories north of the Tana. Thus a vast area, reaching up to the western watershed of the Nile, fell into the British sphere of influence, an influence then exerted by the Imperial British East Africa Company. This company was formed primarily as a trading venture, but by Royal Charter in 1888, it was charged with the administration of this area. Following Germany's withdrawal, therefore, the Company, by agreement with the Sultan of Zanzibar, assumed responsibility, in 1891, for the administration of Jubbaland. What began, then, as a trading venture in Jubbaland ended in a colonial administration, and the Company was vested with political and administrative functions that were beyond its capacity. In 1895 A. H. Hardinge of the British Foreign Office visited the 'Province' and proclaimed the establishment of British colonial rule. From this period Britain created another area out of the Jubbaland, a territory which was later to be known as the Northern Frontier District (NFD).

The need for a refuelling station on the Red Sea to strengthen their naval communication with their Indo-

China and Madagascar dominions led France to gain access to Obok, on the extreme north-west edge of Somaliland territory, establishing a formal French colony and protectorate in 1885, which was to become known as French Somaliland (later Djibouti).

Following an agreement between France and Britain in 1888, the two countries recognised each other's claims to a Protectorate' on the west and east side respectively of the Zeyla to Harar caravan route. This was bound to conflict with Italy's interpretation of the Treaty of Uccialli with Abyssinia. By this treaty Italy acquired, in its view, a protectorate over the whole of Abyssinia. Britain acceded to this view but France contested, and Menelik, for the time being, ignored it.

Menelik's interpretation of the Uccialli Treaty resulted in antagonising Italy, and his relations with France became more cordial. By a concession in 1894 and again in 1896 he permitted France to construct a railway connecting Abyssinia with French Somaliland (Djibouti). On March 1896, tension between Abyssinia and Italy culminated in a confrontation between the two armies at Adowa where the Italians were overwhelmed and out-manoeuvred, resulting in complete victory for Menelik. A peace treaty was signed in the autumn of 1896 in which Italy renounced the Treaty of Uccialli and recognised full sovereignty and independence of Abyssinia.

The Italian defeat at Adowa was a decisive event in the history of the Horn of Africa because it appears to have forced the three European powers to a recognition of Menelik's independence which made it desirable for them to secure from Menelik recognition of their colonial boundaries, without much thought to Menelik's own colonial ambitions.[92] Menelik's victory undid a border agreements which Britain and France had concluded with Italy during this period.

In the middle of nineteenth century the Nile and the Nile valley assumed a major importance within the orbit of the policy framework of Britain and France. Later in 1869 the Abyssinian strategy about the Nile valley dominated the European policy regarding Africa, particularly the Horn. In fact, to buy Menelik's neutrality in the Sudan conflict, Britain concluded border agreement with him in 1897. This treaty, which was concealed from the Somalis, breached the principles of the protectorate which Great Britain concluded with the Somalis.

The original Anglo-Somali Treaties of Protection did not cede any territory to Britain, as had apparently been recognised by the text of the 1897 treaty and annexation of Ethiopia, the British Government now evidently arrived at a new and different interpretation of the position. It was in this way that the Anglo-Ethiopian Agreement of 1954 purported to recognise the sovereignty of Ethiopia over Somali territory, to which it had no prior title.

Nevertheless, Britain decided to surrender Western Somaliland to Ethiopia in fulfillment of the 1942 and 1944 Anglo-Ethiopian Agreements. It is against this background, that on 29 November 1954, an agreement was

---

92 Somali Republic, 1962 16.

concluded between the governments of Great Britain and Ethiopia by which Great Britain transferred the valuable Hawd and Reserved Area (area adjacent to the Ogaden) of Western Somaliland — 67,000 square miles — to Ethiopian administrative control. The agreement terminated the 1944 Agreement which provided for the continuation of the British Military Administration in the Hawd (Haud) and Reserved Areas without prejudice to Ethiopia's sovereignty.[93] Some observers believe that Britain did this to induce Ethiopia to "agree to the colonial arrangements made by Europeans during the period between 1885- 1905".[94]

The year 1897 marked a historical period of the imperial history of Horn of Africa. The Anglo-Ethiopian boundary agreement made in this period was to leave a legacy which plagued the relations between Ethiopia and the Somali Republic. Ethiopia had the only organised government in the Horn in that period.

The British Secretary of State for the Colonies in a statement to the House of Commons said in 1955 that,

"he regretted the Treaty of 1897 ... but, like much that has happened before, it is impossible to undo it".[95]

But it was not until 1934, when AngloEthiopian boundary commission attempted to demarcate the boundary that the British protected Somalis became aware of what had happened.

---

93 Bhardwaj, 1979: 28; Samatar et al, 1987: 89; Lewis, 1980: 58.
94 Bhardwaj, 1979: 29.
95 Issa-Salwe, 1996: 50-2.

Italy, delayed by its internal problems, entered late to 'the African feast as a poor relation'.[96] It created a colony in the Benadir in the south, which was under the suzerainty of the Sultan of Zanzibar. Italy was concerned about the interest shown by the British and the Germans in the north-east part of Somaliland where there were two antagonistic sultanates: the Majerten Sultanate of Boqor Osman and the Hobyo Sultanate of Sultan Yusuf Ali Kenadid. These Sultanates of Majerten and Hobyo had developed diverse and very effective political organisations with measures of centralised authority over relatively large territories.[97]

To dilute the influence of its colonial antagonists, Italy concluded a treaty of protectorate with the Sultanate of Hobyo on 8 February 1889 and, after long resistance, with Boqor Osman on 7 April of the same year. This new deal prompted Germany to object to the treaties, claiming that it had priority over Italy in the area. The case was taken to Berlin, and after having considered Article 34 of the General Act of the Berlin Conference of 1884, the case was ruled in favour of Italy.[98] Nevertheless, to avoid clash of interests, the three main European colonial powers, namely Britain, France and Italy "worked out basic spheres of influence and some boundary agreements".[99]

---

96 Samatar et al, 1987: 129.
97 Issa-Salwe, 1996: 17.
98 Hess, 1966: 24-8.
99 Reisman, 1983: 152-3.

Post-war Outcome

A convention signed in 1908 by Italy and Ethiopia established a commission to set-up the boundary between Somalia and Ethiopia. However, the commission's work could not go ahead because of difference of interpretation of trigonometric points of reference. In 1935, Italy with its locally constituted army, invaded Ethiopia from its Somali territory. This invasion following a series of incidents in the early 1930s, culminated in the Wal-waal (Wal Wal) incident in November 1934, in which Italy and Abyssinia were involved in disputes over their respective interpretations of the 1897 agreement on a common border. With this latest conquest, Italy took control of most of the Horn, from its Eritrean colony on the Red Sea, through Abyssinia to southern Somalialand.

Furthermore, in August 1940, within the context of the Second World War, Italy invaded British Somaliland. It further crossed into Kenya and advanced towards Lake Rudolf. The occupation was short lived, however, as the Allied forces seized Muqdisho on 25 February 1941, and in March advanced to win back British Somaliland. In 1941 all Somali territories (with the exception of French Somaliland which remained under the Vichy rule), were destined to remain under the British flag for nearly a decade.[100]

The Allies reinstalled Haile Selassie as emperor of Ethiopia and soon he began to claim both Eritrea and the Ogaden. Haile

---

100   Issa-Salwe, 40-51.

Selassie maintained that the Somalis were part of the great Ethiopian family. In mid 1956 while touring Qabridaharre, Qallafo and Dhagahbuur, the emperor said:

> "We believe that the Somali people are economically tied with Ethiopia, ... it is difficult for the Somalis to survive outside Ethiopia".[101]

The victorious Allied forces divided the liberated area into British Somaliland, the former Italian Somaliland and Hawd (Haud), which lay south of British Somaliland. British Somaliland and Hawd (Haud) were to remain in the hands of the British.

The fate of the former Italian Somaliland was that of the other Italian colonies of Eritrea, Libya and Cyrenaica. At the end of the war in 1945 at Potsdam Conference the Allies agreed that Italian colonies seized during the war would not be returned to Italy. The responsibility for deciding their disposition fell to the Allied Council of Foreign Ministers, which delegated the Four Powers Commission (which was composed of Britain, USSR, US and France). The Commission was established to investigate the wishes of the former Italian Somaliland, concerning their political future.

The then British Foreign Minster, Ernest Bevin, proposed a plan calling a British-supervised trusteeship over all territory then under military administration and leading to eventual

---

101   Del Boca, 1988: 264-5.

independence for Somalia under one flag. However, Bevin's plan was defeated when the United States and the Soviet Union accused Britain of "seeking its own aggrandisement at the expense of Ethiopia and Italy".[102] Prospect that a communist regime might come to power in Italy explained Soviet concern for Italian interests at that time, and the US supported the Christian Democrats to counter Communist influence in Italy.

The process which would decide the fate of Somalis was developing during June and July 1949. In June 1949 Britain withdraw its project of Greater Somaliland thus removing the last obstacle for Italy to return to Somalia under the UN mandate.

In the meantime, on 21 November 1949 the General Assembly assigned a trusteeship over the former colony to Italy for a period of ten years (beginning 1950) under UN supervision (Resolution 289). The Italian administration was to prepare the Somali territory for independence before the end of 1960.

In the same period negotiations took place between Britain and Ethiopia in which the possible exchange for the port of Zeyla (Zeila) and the Hawd and Reserved Area was discussed, with a view to granting Ethiopia direct access to the sea, while permitting the British administration to remain permanently in charge of the territories in which Somali nomads from the British Somaliland grazed their livestock during part

---

102 Rinehart, 1982: 27-8.

of each year.[103] However, as a result of the Federation of Ethiopia and Eritrea, the Ethiopians had added the coast of Eritrea to their territory, making further negotiations with Britain unnecessary. Another reason could have been France's objection to Ethiopia getting a port which would rival Djibouti.[104] Djibouti and Zeyla are both on the Red Sea.

Nevertheless, Britain decided to surrender the Hawd and Reserved Area (part of the Western Somaliland) to Ethiopia in fulfillment of the 1942 and 1944 Anglo-Ethiopian Agreements. It is against this background, that on 29 November 1954, an agreement was concluded between the governments of Great Britain and Ethiopia by which Great Britain transferred the valuable Hawd and Reserved Area to Ethiopian administrative control. The agreement terminated the 1944 Agreement which provided for the continuation of the British Military Administration in the Hawd (Haud) and Reserved Areas without prejudice to Ethiopia's sovereignty. It also stipulated the rights of the British Somaliland nomads to pasture in the Hawd for fourteen years.[105] However, the agreement was abrogated by Haile Selassie in 1960 following a clash in Danod between Ethiopian police and Somali nomads.

Italy protested following the British ceding of Somali territory to Ethiopia. In response the General Assembly encouraged direct negotiation and, eventually, arbitration. In the 1940s a dispute over the border between the UN's

---

103 Issa-Salwe, 1976: 48.
104 Markakis, 1990: 173.
105 *Ibid.*, 173.

Italian Trusteeship of Somalia and Ethiopia prompted the United Nations to advise Italy and Ethiopia to settle their differences. But Ethiopia, which had already acquired the Ogaden and Hawd through Anglo-Ethiopian agreements, was determined to push its borders even further into Somali territory. Based on its interpretation on the Italo-Ethiopian Agreements of 1897 and 1908, it maintained that the frontier ran to the east near the coast. On the contrary, Italy claimed that the frontier lay to the west of the provisional line.

On 15 December 1950, the General Assembly adopted Resolution 392 (V), which recommended that Ethiopia and Italy proceed to negotiate directly.[106] On 14 December 1954 the General Assembly adopted another resolution (Resolution 854) advising the two parties to settle their disputes.[107] To advise on the matter, the UN appointed an arbitration tribunal led by Trygve Lie, a former UN Secretary-General.

In December 1959 Ethiopia and Somalia (under the UN Trusteeship) agreed that until a final settlement could be reached, the British provisional line should remain in force. This line known as the Candole Line was drawn unilaterally by Britain in 1950.[108]

However, the Italo-Ethiopian negotiation could not be started smoothly as the two countries relations was marred by Italian invasion of Ethiopia in 1935. Rome had instructed

---

106   Castagno, 1959: 386.
107   Del Boca, 1988: 264.
108   *Ibid.*, 260-1.

the Italian administration in Muqdisho not to pursue the frontier problem relentlessly.[109] In 1952 the two countries resumed diplomatic relations. From 1952 to 1954, Italy avoided to face the frontier problems. The two parties did not meet until 1956.

The contentious issue was the interpretation of the Italo-Ethiopian agreement. In Article 1 it stated that the delineation of the frontiers between Italian colony and Ethiopia must be stipulated by international agreement. Italy insisted that any agreement should be made in consideration of the local people. On the contrary, Ethiopia maintained that the agreement must be interpreted according to the 1897 treaty.[110] The Italo-Ethiopian negotiation met a setback when on 29 November 1954 Britain transferred Hawd and the Reserved Area's control to Ethiopia. When in 1960 Somalia gained its independence there was no *de facto* border between Somalia and Ethiopia.

THE SOCIO-ECONOMIC FACTOR

Other causes of the Horn of Africa conflict can be said to be socio-economic factors which extend in almost the entire Horn of Africa. This is reflected in the conflict between the Muslim lowlander pastoral population with the Christian highlander agriculturists.[111] The colonisers settlements in

---

109   *Ibid.*, 261.
110   *Ibid.*, 264.
111   Bhardwaj, 1979: 2.

the Horn concentrated in the agriculture area of the region. Christianised people living there benefited from these developments. The result was underdevelopment of the lowlands under the colonisers and later by the post-colonial masters in Kenya, Ethiopia (including Eritrea) "accentuated the deep-seated and long drawn-out rivalries"[112] between the nomadic Muslim lowlanders and the peasant Christian highlanders. This legacy was to become a base for future conflict.

Bhardwaj observes that other consequences of underdevelopment have been the weakening of national cohesion and the birth of powerful centrifugal, tribal and regional forces. According to him,

"... the rival systems of nationalism in the Horn area are the outcome of a long suppressed resentment against the colonial plunder and post-colonial elitist strategy of economic development".[113]

The first post-colonial government did not make much effort to ease the plight of the nomadic peoples in Eritrea, Ethiopia as well as in Kenya.

The religion and economic underdevelopment and ingredients of the Horn conflict, have been intensified by the global situation as it became a platform of rivalry between

---

112   Ibid., 2.
113   Ibid., 2.

the two superpowers, later presented as ideological conflict. However, the internationalisation of the conflict was not ideological, but rather strategic and military. To protect themselves from outside — and their internal enemies — the rival countries of the Horn have sought external help. This in turn developed the Horn into a strategic area for Eastern and Western blocs to compete.

Chapter Five

SOMALI NATIONALISM AND FRONTIER REVISION

Developing outside the main stream of African thinking, Somali nationalism is also based on an ethnic-cultural nationhood embracing all Somalis — those living in the Somali Republic as well as those in Kenya, Ethiopia, and the French Somaliland. As a state, the Somali Republic has acted as a pole of attraction to the Somalis living outside its boundaries. It has actively pursued irredentist policies and encouraged separatism among the Somalis of Kenya and Ethiopia (and Djibouti). It could afford to pursue an irredentist policy because it is a nation-state. As the legitimising principle of the Somali state was Somali nationhood, it could not settle for the *status quo* norm.

While most African leaders were engaged in a policy of developing a set of values and ideas that all citizens of the new state would share, Somali leaders were faced with a reverse problem to their African counterparts. Their nationalism, in what Lewis says, "was tailor-made", and their problem was not that of nation-building within the inherited borders, but of extending statehood outside the frontiers of the Somali Republic to embrace the remaining portions of the nation. Many people who lived in countries bordering Somalia would rather live under the jurisdiction of the Somali state.

At the end of the nineteenth century Eastern Africa experienced resurgence of Islam as a result of its revival in the Muslim world. This tendency might have been triggered by the Euro-Christian colonisation of Muslim lands in Africa and Asia, creating a widespread reaction culminating in the rise of a revivalist movement to oppose the Euro-Christian hegemony. The Mahdist revolt in the Sudan in closing of the nineteenth century and that of the Dervish movement led by Sayid Mahamed in Somaliland during the same period are examples of this revivalist movement.[114]

The Somali reaction to alien domination was always aggressive and served to emphasise a Somali common identity. Inspired by this cause the Dervish movement led by Sayid Mahamed Abdulle Hassan (since early 1920s) fought for two decades against Britain, Italy and Ethiopia's intrusion in Somaliland. Modern Somali nationalism was inspired by Dervish movement.

---

114   Issa-Salwe, 1996: 24-5.

The Somali flag is a five-pointed white star set in a field of azure blue. The star is the proud symbol of irredentist nationalism. Its five points represent the five territories which Somalis are endeavouring to integrate into a Greater Somalia. These territories--the Somali-inhabited region of the Ogaden, the Northern Frontier District (presently North-Eastern province of Kenya) and Djibouti (former French Somaliland) are to become parts of the Somali nation-state (see map).

The Somali claim contains all the ingredients of "classical" irredentism, including ethnic fragments across the borders and organised nationalist movements struggling to achieve unification with the "mother country".[115] They perceive the Somali nation in Somalia, Ethiopia, Kenya and Djibouti as one "organic" whole. Underlying the demand for a Greater Somalia is the strong feeling that all Somalis are one nation.

The pan-Somali ideology was nurtured by a feeling of national consciousness which focuses on the shared heritage of Islam, belief in a common ancestor, language and culture and, in addition, the geographical continuity of the areas they inhabit. Somalia insisted on Somalis in Ethiopia and Kenya (and Djibouti which was under French control until mid 1977) to exercise the right to self-determination; it was hoped they would then opt out of those states and eventually join with the Somali Republic.[116]

---

115 Neuberger, 1991: 98.
116 Farah, 1993: 83-4.

Somalia's Territorial Claims

The territory that Somalia claimed in Ethiopia is sizeable, amounting to one fifth of Ethiopia's whole. It also claimed the Northern Frontier District (NFD), at present North-Eastern Province of Kenya. The dispute of Somalia against its neighbours is regarded as involving "core values" concerning the definition of the "national self".

In reaction to Somalia's aim, Kenya and Ethiopia felt that the Somali claim challenged their survival as states. They considered the problem of ethnic Somalis in their respective countries not as a question of the right to self-determination, but rather as one of the territorial integrity of the post-colonial state. Any idea contrary to that, they believed, could create a centrifugal force which could threaten their statehood.

In a memorandum presented by the Kenyan delegation at the inaugural OAU conference in 1963 in Addis Ababa, Kenya reiterated that principle of self-determination was applicable only to where foreign domination continued. In response to the Somali threat Ethiopia and Kenya concluded a mutual defence pact in 1964.

From the outset the OAU faced the problem of artificial colonial-imposed boundaries. The issue was particularly acute where, as in Somalia, these boundaries divided people belonging to the same ethnic group. In both the first and second All-Africa People's Conference there was a mood favouring revision of the boundaries. A resolution echoing Somali case had been adopted. However, the OAU member states shelved the sensitive border problems in 1963. Before the end of that year fighting broke out between Morocco and Algeria, and between Somalia and its neighbouring states, Ethiopia and Kenya.

At its second summit held in Cairo in July 1964, the OAU complicated the whole issue by accepting that all borders should remain as they were when the colonial powers left Africa. Somalia stood out in rejecting the OAU position that approved colonial borders. President Adan Abdulle Osman of Somalia had presented his case at the May 1963 meeting:

> Briefly the Somali problem is this: unlike any other border problem in Africa, the entire length of the existing boundaries, as imposed by the colonialists, cut across the traditional pastures of our nomadic population. The problem becomes unique when it is realised that no other nation in Africa finds itself totally divided along the whole length of its borders from its own people.[117]

A large number of the Somali people remained outside the boundaries handed over to Somalia by the colonial powers. Samatar and Laitin describe the situation as follows:

> "The most unfortunate consequence of Somali history for current politics is the fact that a significant percentage of those who are part of the Somali tradition do not live within the boundaries handed to Somalis by the colonial powers. Many of them still

---

117   Tordoff, 1990: 250.

live as second class citizens in Kenya and as unwanted subjects in Ethiopia. Many straddle the borders and rely on water holes and grassland on both sides. This difficult situation has added to the pathos of the story of contemporary Somali politics [because of] the significance of this issue of boundaries, and a deep desire of so many Somalis to be united under the flag of a single state".[118]

The newly independent African states felt unequal to tackling the disorder of land and people that the colonialists had left behind. For the Somalis, however, it represented the legitimisation of an African state colonising another.

This was a matter of life and death for the Somalis. For example, the Ogaden region is an integral part of the pastoralist economy. Acceptance of OAU position could limit the movement of pastoralists to and from Western Somaliland. The area is rich in pasture in the rainy seasons

— April to June and October to November — and the animals do not need much water as they get moisture from the green leaves. However, in the dry season the pastoralists would migrate with their animals to eastern Somalia where water is more abundant. Curbing their movements leaves the pastoralists vulnerable, as this pattern of movement is the time tested traditional response to drought.[119] A longer term consequence for the environment is deforestation and

---

118   Samatar et al, 1987: 64.
119   Raikes, ed., 1990: 31.

desertification, the result of over grazing. In the words of Louis Fitzgibbon,

"The Ogaden is a featureless expanse of desert and scrub. But to the Somali nomad pastoralists it is 'home', notwithstanding its meagre resources with respect to water and grazing. Its security was promised by the British colonialists after the 'scramble for Africa'. Yet it was they who, between 1890 and 1954 gave it away, piece by piece, to Abyssinia, the traditional enemy of the Somalis. It was that betrayal that has led to a century of suffering and strife, as well as death".[120]

ATTEMPTS TO SOLVE THE DISPUTES

At the end of 1962 a tentative step to solve Somalia's dispute with its neighbours was the idea to create a confederation alliance in East Africa. In addition to Uganda, Kenya, and Tanganyika (later Tanzania, when it joined with Zanzibar), the East Africa Federation was to include Somalia and Ethiopia. This scheme was to come under the East African Association, which was to be expanded to become the East African Common Services Organisation (EACSO).

However, the hope that a confederation might neutralise the territorial dispute between Somali and its neighbours was dashed when Somalia opposed federation before boundary revision. Prime Minister Sharmarke, while responding to this proposal in August 1962 to Ronald Ngala, KADU leader, said:

---

120   Fitzgibbon, "The Ogaden" war video comment.

The Somali Republic, though otherwise more than willing to do so [confederate], can only enter into a political federation on the prior condition that the constituent part, comprising all Somalis who wish to be reunited, is established before the Republic enter into the proposed federal relationship.[121]

SOMALIA'S DISPUTE WITH ETHIOPIA

The Western Somaliland (known also as Ogaden) dispute was a rivalry involving the aspirations and claims of two very different types of nationalism. Both Somalia and Ethiopia had strong sense of nationalism which predated the colonial era. While Somalia's nationalism was largely ethnic and culture based on the homogeneity of the Somali people, Ethiopia's nationalism was "fundamentally political, based on the legacy of the Ethiopian Empire as the oldest independent country in Africa".[122] Ethiopia strengthened its claims on the basis that its emperors held suzerainty over the Ogaden as a result of boundary agreement signed with the Italians and the British.[123]

While Ethiopia calls the region Ogaden, Somalia recognises it as Western Somaliland. The former, however, does not reflect the whole territory which Somalia claims.

To separate the region from Somali identity, Ethiopia named the region Ogaden, a name which indicated simple one of the Ethiopian-Somali ethnic peoples. Ogaden clan

---

121 Touval, 1972: 214-215.
122 Porter, 1984: 186.
123 *Ibid.*, 187.

is one of the major Somali clans who live in the region (it can also be found among all the main Somali clan groups). Administratively, the Ogaden makes part of the Hararghe Province and stretches from Jigjiga, the region's capital, to the Somali border, a territory exclusively inhabited by ethnic Somalis. In this sense the Ogaden makes roughly two thirds of the territory which Somalia recognises as Western Somaliland. For Somalia, however, Western Somaliland stretches from Awash Valley in the north-west (just 150 miles from Addis Ababa) round the periphery of the Ethiopian highlands to the east until the Somali border and Moyale in the West. Touching Kenya, Ethiopia and Somali borders, the Somali-Ethiopian border stretches to the north until it meets with Djibouti borders.

Western Somaliland constitutes one fifth of Ethiopia's area as it covers 200,000 square kilometres with a population estimated to be about one million. In spite of the fact that there are similarities between the Western Somaliland and NFD disputes, the border between Ethiopia and Somalia has never been delineated clearly.[124] Instead, the border between Somalia and Kenya was created as a result of unilateral act of one government, in this case by Britain.

When Somalia gained independence, its frontier with Ethiopia was still, in the international law, a "provisional" border. From the Somali perspective apparently the Ogaden and NFD case differ. Since the border between Ethiopia and Somalia had never been delineated clearly, Somalia felt that

---

124 Samatar et al, 1987: 135.

it had better chances to get boundary revision than in its dispute with Kenya. While successive Somali governments never ceased to campaign for all its missing territories, they have spent more resources and energy to the liberation of the Ogaden than the other missing territories.

Clashes began in the Hawd (in the Ogaden) within six months after Somali independence. This followed a small skirmish involving Somali nomads and Ethiopian border police. These incidents were regular occurrences until in January 1964 armed conflict between Somali and Ethiopian regular armed troops erupted along the entire length of the Somali-Ethiopian frontier. Open hostilities were brought to an end the following month through the meditation of the Sudanese President, Ibrahim Abboud, acting under the auspices of the OAU.[125]

THE BACKGROUND OF THE SOMALI-ETHIOPIAN BOUNDARY DISPUTE

As previously mentioned, the problems of the boundary between Somalia and Ethiopia was an inheritance of Italian and Ethiopian expansions over the arid lowlands of the Somali-inhabited region. A dispute over the border between the UN's Italian Trusteeship (which governed Italian Somaliland) and Ethiopia in the 1940s prompted the United Nations to advise Italy and Ethiopia to settle their differences peacefully. While, Ethiopia, maintained that the frontier ran to the east

---

125   Rinehart, 1982: 39.

near the coast, Italy claimed that the frontier lay to the west of the provisional line.

The territory administrated by the Italian administration between 1920 to 1935, extended in the south from the coast inward to approximately the present frontier: From FeerFeer- (Fer-fer) northward to the border of British Somaliland, at 8° North and 47° East, the line wandered for about 180 miles from the coastline.

Between 1935 and 1950 Italy and later Britain administered the Ogaden as integral part of Somalia. In 1950 Britain established a "provisional administrative boundary" and placed the northern section of the line farther east than the limits of pre-1935 Italian occupation.

To advise on the matter, the UN appointed an arbitration tribunal led by Mr Trygve Lie, a former UN Secretary-General. However, in December 1959 Ethiopia and Somalia (under the UN Trusteeship) agreed that until a final settlement could be reached, the British provisional line should remain in force. Following two visits to the Trust Territory in 1951 and 1954, the United Nations Visiting Mission to Italian Somaliland reported the growing concern over the issue of frontier situation. A report which the mission compiled in 1951 reads as following:

It would be unfortunate if, in addition to the many serious problems which will unavoidably exist as the trusteeship arranged likewise inherits an unresolved boundary question.[126]

---

126 Castagno, 1959: 387.

In its 1954 report, the Advisory Council paid considerable attention to the Somali reaction over Britain's transfer of the Hawd and Reserved Area, which until then Britain administered as part of the British Somaliland.

When in 1960 Somalia gained its independence the territorial issue was still pending, thus making the Western Somaliland case not a firm boundary dispute but, in the eyes of international law, a provisional disagreement.[127]

Post-Colonial Era

When in 1960 Somalia gained independence there was no *de facto* border between Somalia and Ethiopia. Obviously, Somalia's case was obscured by the diplomatic and historical power of Ethiopia. Although Ethiopia is, in Lewis opinion "essentially a traditional, pluralist African conquest state"[128], in the African eyes it was a symbol of Black Power. Having defeated a Italian colonial army at Adowa in 1896, Ethiopia was set to share with the European powers the spoils of the territory of the Horn of Africa. It established its present frontiers by participating with the European colonial powers in the partition of Africa. Mussolini's failed plan to create an Italian East African empire further enhanced Ethiopia's chance to get the sympathy of the allies.

Ethiopia's special status and its being a pluralist state, was a recipe for African leaders to accept the Ethiopian principle

---

127 Samatar et al, 1987: 132.
128 Lewis, 1980: 56

of territorial integrity of all African states. Ethiopia was also instrumental in creating the OAU and that was another major influence.

While OAU applied the principle of legitimisation of the inherited colonial boundaries, which is enshrined in the Charter of the OAU as *Article 3(3)*, it refused to apply the other relevant principle in the Somali case, *Article 3(6)*, which declared the principle of absolute dedication to the total emancipation of African territories which are still dependent.[129] Nevertheless, African leaders preferred the Ethiopian version which otherwise could expose Ethiopia as an imperial power. African leaders have shown little concern to see Somali dispute as a self-determination issue meriting serious attention and sympathy.[130]

The Somalis insisted that the inviolability of frontiers applied to sovereign but not colonial states, and that since Ethiopia was a colonial state, the Somalis in Western Somaliland had the same right to rebel against colonial authority. Whatever the historical plausibility of the Somali thesis, the OAU could have not jeopardise its own existence by reclassifying one of its founding member states as a colonial power.

In the meantime, to foment hostility in the Ogaden and NFD, and make the Somali inhabited regions ungovernable, the Somali government adopted the strategy to help the local

---

129   Samatar et al, 1987: 131.
130   Lewis, 1980: vi.

people. This coincided with the formation of the Western Somali Liberation Front (WSLF) on 16 June 1963 at Hodayo in Ethiopia. The group began their campaign by launching a rebellion against the Ethiopian rule. Consequently, the Ethiopian government reinforced their hold on the main administrative centres.

Meanwhile, in Kenya the *shifta,* the name given to the NFD Liberation Front activists, began to destabilise the region. In reaction the Kenyan government ruled the region with iron fist; the region was brought under what Farah calls "the punitive steering of Chapter 57 of the Laws of Kenya".[131]

Ethiopia's Claims

Ethiopia claimed Eritrea and Somalia after Second World War; it argued that these two countries were part of Ethiopia in historic times. However, with the advent of African states to independence, Ethiopia dropped its previous attitude and became an ardent supporter of the *status quo*. The change was believed to have been influenced by the ethnic basis of Somali irredentism.

In 1941, after Ethiopia's liberation from Italian rule, Haile Selassie talked about the restoration of Benadir region (the name Ethiopian use to call Somalia) to historical Ethiopia. An imperial proclamation of 1941 declared:

---

131   Farah, 1993: 85-6.

I have come to restore the independence of my country, including Eritrea and the Benadir, whose people will henceforth dwell under the shade of the Ethiopian flag.[132]

In 1949 he extended his ambitions and demanded the incorporation of the whole of Somaliland into the Ethiopian Empire. In 1960 the claim was dropped, but the Ethiopian emperor observed that "things would have been quite different according to history", thus indirectly maintaining the historical claim. Next to its historical demand for Somali territory, Ethiopia's claims are based, in international law, upon the 1897 Treaty. From the Somali point of view, however, the May 14, 1897 Treaty was not a valid treaty. It claimed that the Anglo-Somali Treaties of Protection of 1884-1889 (which preceded the Anglo- Ethiopian Agreement) did not give to Britain authority to transfer. Thus, in ceding Somali territory to the other party, Britain violated the agreements which it had concluded with the Somali clans. The treaty violated the "fundamental trust which was expressed in the Protectorate Agreements on which the British rested their authority with regard to the Somali territory".[133] According to Reisman, in cases of inhabited territory, the first authority is the will of the indigenous inhabitants.[134] Therefore, in international law the basic authority in the disposition of Somali territory is to be by applying the principle of self-determination.

---

132 Reisman, 1983: 153.
133 Reisman, 1983: 158; Rinehart, 1982: 39.
134 *Ibid.*, 160.

Somali-Ethiopian Diplomatic Contact

Prior to the Somali independence, the first contact between Ethiopia and Italian Somaliland took place in 1957, when Adan Abdulle Osman, the then president of the Somali National Assembly (and later president of the Republic, 1960-1967), and Abdullahi Issa (then prime minister) paid a visit to Addis Ababa. Although the talks failed to bridge the gap between the two countries, it ended on a note of goodwill. Following Somalia's independence in 1960, the two countries established diplomatic relations and held many talks.

The Somali-Ethiopian dispute came up for discussion at the Monrovia conference in May 1961 and at the African summit conference in Addis Ababa in May 1963.[135] Although the meeting provided an opportunity for the two parties to talk to each other, relations between them did not improve.

Following a series of guerrilla activities in Ethiopia at the end of January 1964 there developed a clash between the Somali and Ethiopian regular armies. On 9 February, Somalia requested both the UN Security Council and the OAU to look into the matter. It pledged the Security Council to send a commission to the area to ascertain the responsibility for the fighting and to supervise any eventual cease fire. Somalia asked for the creation of a demilitarised zone along the border. The position of neutral observers in this area was to get an international recognition that the Somali-inhabited area of Ethiopia and Kenya — over which these two states claimed

---

135 Touval, 1972: 213.

exclusive sovereignty — were actually disputed territories.¹³⁶ This objective was more likely to be achieved through placing the issue before the UN Security Council than by referring it to the OAU. The posting of observers was supported by Ghana, Libya, Tunisia, Nigeria and Congo-Brazzaville.¹³⁷

For its part, Ethiopia asked for an extraordinary session of the OAU Council of Ministers to consider the dispute.¹³⁸ On February 12, the Council of Ministers met in Dar-es-Salaam, and secured a pledge from both parties to refrain from appealing to other international organisations, while the matter was being looked into by the OAU. Somalia was not keen to accept the appeal. Morocco, which had been reluctant to submit its territorial dispute with Algeria to international arbitration, supported Somalia.

U Thant, the UN Secretary-General, shared the idea that the OAU should look into African disputes before they reach the UN. However, Somalia feared that the OAU could be prejudiced against its cause.¹³⁹

At the Council of Ministers reconciliation meeting at Dar-es-Salaam, both Ethiopia and Kenya preferred the OAU than UN to debate the matter. While Somalia refused to be drawn into the discussion of the wider issue, both Ethiopia and Kenya asked the Council to discuss the political roots

---

136   *Ibid.*, 218.
137   *Ibid.*, 219.
138   *Ibid.*, 216-217.
139   *Ibid.*, 213.

of the dispute and the question of principle involved, and to find a permanent solution on the basis of respect for the territorial integrity of states and the acceptance of existing borders. They expected that the presence of all African states would have been more damaging to Somalia than "a rebuff by the Security Council".[140] It was only when a compromise formula which was conceived by Somalia to postpone its appeal to the UN that gave the OAU a chance to look into the matter.

The Security Council adopted a resolution referring to the question of jurisdiction over African disputes, proclaiming that "the Unity of Africa requires the solution to all disputes between Member States be sought first within the Organisation of African Unity".[141] It also called for a cease-fire, the cessation of hostile propaganda, and negotiations for a peaceful settlement of the dispute.

Under the auspices of General Ibrahim Abboud, the Sudanese president, in March 1964, a meeting between the Somali and Ethiopian foreign ministers in Khartoum became unexpectedly successful when agreements were reached for the "maintenance of the cease-fire, the creation of demilitarised zone along the borders, the establishment of a joint commission to supervise the withdrawal of forces, and the cessation of hostile propaganda".[142] With the blessing of the OAU, the parties agreed to resume negotiations before

---

140 *Ibid.*, 218
141 *Ibid.*, 218-9.
142 *Ibid.*, 221.

the next meeting of the OAU Assembly of Heads of State and Government.

By the end of 1964 and the beginning of 1965 Somalia was satisfied that the world was aware of the Somali dispute. The *National Review,* published by the Somali Ministry of Information, stated:

> For the first time in recent history, the existence of a problem along Somalia's borders had been openly recognised at an international level... So Africa and the world now know that the rightful claim of the Somalis still under foreign rule must be accepted before there can be a just and permanent peace in East Africa, and the OAU Charter becomes a reality.[143]

In spite of the Somali's jubilant progress, Kenya's and Ethiopia's diplomatic moves led to an outcome where Somalia could be isolated at the end.

SOMALIA'S DISPUTE WITH KENYA

The Northern Frontier District (present North-Eastern Province of Kenya) represented the second dispute that arose from Somali irredentist aspirations. NFD comprised three separate administrative districts: Wajer, Garisa and Mandera. At least 60 percent of NFD's population consider themselves Somalis, and most of the others are people, like the Oromo, who are ethnically related to the Somalis. Somalis inhabit almost the whole of the eastern part of the region. Marked

---

143   *Ibid.*, 221.

by the Somali-line which ran southwards from the east of Moyale to the Tana River, the demarcation was created by the British administration to separate the Somali pastoral nomads from their ethnic kinsmen, the Orma, Sakuye, Gabra, and Rendille.

Relations with Kenya were slightly different. Until the 1940s, the NFD was isolated from the influence of modern economy as the British colonial office administrated this region as a separate entity. This was because of "concern with security and economy" by the British military administration.[144] As the region was not well enough endowed for agricultural entrepreneur, the administration saw the area not fit for profitable investment. In 1926 the military administration declared the area a Closed District and Special District in 1934; the region remained untouched by the developments "that were transforming the African communities on the Kenyan highlands".[145]

Despite the pan-Somali wave which reached these parts at the end of the 1940s, political activities remained dormant until the 1960s when the British administration lifted a ban on political organisations. In the new situation, the Somalis could express their willingness and determination whether or not to join their kinsmen in the Somali Republic. New political parties also emerged. With the change in British attitude, the Somali Republic became optimistic about British acceptance of the will of its subjects.

---

144   Markakis, 1990: 182
145   *Ibid.*, 182.

To meet these new developments in November 1961, the Somali National Assembly passed a resolution which could pave the way for NFD to join the mother country. The political momentum in the region received new momentum with the motion. In the following year, at the Kenya Constitutional Conference held in Lancaster House in London, the NFD delegation firmly voiced their desire to be granted an autonomous status that would eventually help union with the Somali Republic.[146]

THE NORTHERN FRONTIER DISTRICT ISSUE

Somalia insisted that colonial powers had the responsibility to settle any dispute concerning it. It argued that the British government had the responsibility to arrange for the exercise of self-determination in the NFD. Britain advised Somalia to discuss the matter with the Kenyan nationalist leaders.

At the invitation of Somalia, in July and August 1962 (one year before Kenya's independence) leaders of the Kenya's two major parties, Jomo Kenyatta, leader of Kenya African National Union (KANU) and Ronald Ngala of Kenya African Democratic Union (KADU) visited Somalia separately. Both political leaders opposed the separation of the NFD. Kenyatta further insisted that "the NFD problem was a domestic Kenyan affair in which Somalia was not to interfere".[147]

---

146   Farah, 1993:38.
147   Touval, 1972: 213-4.

In reaction, the Somali Prime Minister, Abdirashiid Ali Sharmarke, responded angrily by reiterating that,

"... any external opposition to Somali reunification is considered as interference in the domestic affairs of the Somali people".[148]

The major diplomatic test for Kenya came some time in May 1963, at the inaugural conference of the Organisation of African Unity in Addis Ababa. Although Kenya was not an independent state at the time, Kenyan delegate attended the conference in the capacity of an observer-delegate. The delegate presented his position on the Somali claims in this way:

The principle of self-determination has relevance where foreign domination is the issue. It has no relevance where the issue is territorial disintegration by dissident citizens.[149]

To ease the tension between Somalia and Kenya, the British Colonial Secretary at the time, Reginald Maulding, announced the appointment of a commission to survey the opinion of the people in NFD.[150] The commission's findings based on a survey held in October 1962, were that the majority of the population favoured joining the Somali Republic. In the conclusion of its report and with the regard to its findings in the Somali area, the Commission reported:

---

148   *Ibid.*, 214.
149   Farah, 1993: 84.
150   Farah, 1993 :37.

As we have already said, the Somali delegations seen by us in these areas [NFD] were unanimous in their desire not to be included in any region of Kenya. Apart from one of these delegations, which wished the area to remain under the British control for the time, all these delegations wished the Northern Frontier District to be joined with the Somali Republic.[151]

Following the report, on 6 January 1963 the Somali Republic formally sent advice to the British government which stated that the Somali Republic,

> "...[was] prepared to accept as its own duty the assumption of sovereignty over the territory and people in question".[152]

In an attempt to play down Somali government's concern, on 11 February, Britain assured that "it would be consulted before any final decision is taken on the future of NFD".[153] However, by failing to honour its promise, and contrary to the wishes of its subjects, Britain instead announced on 8 March 1963 that NFD was to be brought into Kenya's regional constitution. The British Colonial and Commonwealth Secretary Duncan Sandys announced in Nairobi that,

---

151 Farah, 1993: 81.
152 Touval, 1972: 184.
153 *Ibid.*, 184.

"... NFD would form one of the regions into which Kenya would be divided, and that its Somali population would enjoy a wide measure of autonomy within this framework".[154]

In reaction on 11 March 1963, the Somali Republic broke off diplomatic ties with Britain. The British decision reflected a desire not to endanger its relations with the new Commonwealth country of Kenya. Britain concentrated more on its future relations than on honouring its commitments and responsibilities over its subjects.

Other reasons which made Britain to ignore the outcome of survey is said to be that it felt the federal format then proposed in the Kenya constitution would provide a solution through the degree of autonomy it allowed the predominant Somali region within the federal system.[155]

The Aftermath

On 1 June 1963 Britain transferred to Kenyan leaders some responsibilities, such as that of the internal affairs. Despite the diplomatic rupture between Somalia and Britain, Kenya's leaders continued to be a channel for communication between Somalia and Kenya. In August 1963 Somalia, Britain and Kenya met in Rome on the question of the Northern Frontier District.[156] Somalia proposed a formula which would place

---

154   *Ibid.*, 184.
155   Rinehart, 1982: 38-9.
156   Touval, 1972: 184-5.

NFD under a special administration. Such administration should be either: (i) a joint Somali/Kenya administration, or (ii) to be placed under United Nations administration.[157]

Britain rejected any idea which would involve changing the frontiers of Kenya before independence. It also declared that "the Kenya Government recognises the interest of Somalia in the future of any people of Somali origin residing in Kenya".[158] The talks failed. Neither side was prepared to compromise its position.

KENYAN-SOMALI DIPLOMATIC CONTACT

In spite of these differences contact between Somalia and Kenya leaders continued. On 12 December 1963 Kenya got independence. And in December 1965, President Julius Nyerere of Tanzania tried to open a dialogue between Kenya and Somalia in Arusha, but the rift between the two nations impeded all means of resolving the issue and led instead to their diplomatic rupture on 21 June 1966.

To tighten its internal security, the Kenyan government took drastic security measures and ordered that whoever was to be found sympathetic to the shifta (the name given to the NFD Liberation Front activists) should be imprisoned for life and their property confiscated. The whole of the Somali inhabited area was brought under, what Farah calls

---

157　Ibid., 184.
158　Ibid., 185.

"the punitive steering of Chapter 57 of the Laws of Kenya".[159] The law gave extraordinary power to members of the security forces and administration officers.

In spite of the two countries confronting each other in fierce diplomatic rounds, their armies never clashed. During the Ogaden war, Kenyan border troops were in full alert in case of invasion by Somali armies. However, during the height of the Ogaden War in 1978 things changed quickly when, on 29 June 1978, 3000 Somali troops while trying to cross through Kenyan border near Ramu were confronted by the Kenyan police forces. In the skirmish, the Kenyan police were overrun by the better armed Somali troops. In the ensuing diplomatic war, the Somali government played down the Ramu issue.

SOMALIA'S DISPUTE WITH FRANCE

Djibouti, which before its independence was known as French Somaliland (France changed it to French Territory of Afar and Ises later) represents the fifth point on the Somali star. Covering an area of 23,000 square kilometres, Djibouti is also the third dispute that arose from Somali irredentist aspirations. The population of this tiny territory belong to the Issa Somalis and Afar — both groups belong to the Eastern Cushitic ethnic group. While both groups' habitations extend inside Ethiopia, the Issa Somalis stretch

---

159   Farah, 1993: 85-6.

to the east into northern Somalia, the Afar live along the Danakil coast reaching Massawa in Eritrea.

Ethiopia claimed that the Afars were part of their empire. However, apart from a nominal suzerainty over the Afars, there is no evidence that the Afars were part of the Ethiopia empire. The first Arabian adventurers who crossed the Bab-el-Mandeb found that the peoples of the Horn of Africa were tributaries of the kingdom of Awdal (Adal), with its capital at Zeyla (Zeila) which is now in Somalia. This kingdom was associated with smaller groups in Arabia until the third century BC when it seems to have been subjected to considerable pressure from Abyssinia.[160]

Harar which was built in the sixteenth century, soon became the richest town in East Africa, an independent city-state, and a center of commerce and of Islamic learning.[161] In February 1887 after many attempts Menelik and his army commander, Ras Waldo Gabriel, finally defeated Emir Abdullahi of Harar at Ghalauko.[162]

Sandwiched between Ethiopia and Somalia, the French Somaliland was complicated by the Ethiopia and Somalia competition for the territory. Somalia and Ethiopia pursued different tactics. While Somalia's claim was based on ethnic reason, Ethiopia's was an economic one. With the exception of its access through Eritrea (Eritrea now is an independent state),

---

160 Bhardwaj, 1979: 120-130.
161 Trimingham, 1952: 140-150.
162 *Ibid.*, 150.

Ethiopia was considered a land locked country. It needed Djibouti port and Haile Selassie would not countenance French Somaliland being ceded to Somalia. In spite of the Ethiopian-Somali war of 1977-1978 being concentrated on the Ogaden region, it was Djibouti which lay in the background of the war. The conflict led to an abrupt stoppage of the Addis-Djibouti railway, throwing the entire Djibouti economy and Ethiopia's external trade into disarray. The political and military hurricane of the Horn of Africa had submerged Djibouti.

The Somali strategy on Djibouti was different from its other tactics as this was raised as a question of decolonisation. Somalia insisted that the territory ought to be placed under the United Nations or OAU control. However, the United Nations Committee on Colonialism (Committee of Twenty Four) preferred to treat the matter cautiously.

In 1963 OAU established the OAU Liberation Committee to deal with the last European colonial bastions in the African continent. The committee was charged with co-ordinating aid to liberation movements in the continent. The committee first placed on the agenda the decolonisation of the French Somaliland in June 1963.[163]

The Somali-Ethiopian competition over the territory was heightened when, in August 1966, Charles de Gaulle, while on a visit to Djibouti, was greeted by demonstrations for independence and anti-colonial slogans. And in reaction de

---

163 Touval, 1972: 226.

Gaulle announced a referendum in which the people could express "in a democratic way" their wish to remain (or not) as "a part of France".[164]

At the request of Somalia, in November 1966 the question of French Somaliland was placed on the agenda of OAU conference. Somalia and the more radical African states pressed for unequivocal endorsement of independence for Djibouti and that the referendum be supervised by the OAU or the United Nations.

OAU members faced a dilemma with the question of Djibouti as the subject could heighten the confrontation between Ethiopia and Somalia. Some delegates were concerned that France's withdrawal might result in a serious confrontation between Ethiopia and Somalia. Haile Selassie indicated that if France withdrew from the territory Ethiopia would occupy it. As landlocked country Ethiopia felt threatened if Djibouti would join Somalia. Haile Selassie declared that,

> "[Ethiopia] will never accept a solution ... which is in contradiction to the interest of the people concerned and in violation of the rights of the Ethiopian people".[165]

On October 31, the Liberation Committee adopted a resolution calling on the population to vote for independence in the forthcoming referendum. Nonetheless, the Council of

---

164 Lewis, 1980: 57.
165 Touval, 1972: 227.

Ministers refused to endorse the text. Finally, on November 4 a compromise was reached which reflected the cautious attitude of the majority of states. The resolution expressed that the referendum should be "free", "democratic" and "impartial".

While failing to persuade OAU to call for international supervision of the plebiscite, Somalia won the United Nations General Assembly support when on December 21, 1966 United Nations General Assembly adopted a resolution calling for international supervision for the plebiscite. However, the issue divided African states opinion. Fifteen states, Ethiopia among them, abstained from voting, while twenty states, among them Kenya, voted for it.[166]

The Djibouti case created sympathy for Somalia among some African states. This was in sharp contrast to the isolation in which Somalia found itself during the OAU's debate over the issue of Somalia's disputes with Kenya and Ethiopia.

The referendum took place on 19 March 1967, without the supervision of the United Nations, the Organisation of African Unity or any other international observer. The outcome, as announced by the French authority, was that 60% of the inhabitants of French Somaliland voted to remain as "part of France". Ethiopia accepted the outcome, while Somalia claimed fraud and called for an investigation of the "manner in which the referendum was conducted".[167] To clear

---

166   Ibid., 229.
167   Issa-Salwe, 1996: 69.

the influence of the Somali nationalism, the French colonial office changed French Somaliland's name to the French Territory of the Afars and Ises. To drive a wedge between the two communities of Afar and Issa Somalis, the French government took measures to promote the Afar community. In fact, by this time a clear division was eventually surfacing in the political interests of the two main communities.

In June 1977, France gave the territory independence and to deter any attempt from both Ethiopia and Somalia, it left in its former colony a military legionnaire and a naval power. France's naval presence also served the West's strategic interest in the region. Lying at the mouth of Bab-el-Mandeb, Djibouti became an important strategic place.

Somalia's Diplomatic Tactics

In mid 1965 the Somali government began to review its policy towards its neighbours. This period coincided with a change of government when in September 1964 President Adan Abdulle Osman dismissed his Prime Minster, Dr Sharmarke, and called Abdirisaq Haji Husein to form a new government. Premier Abdirisaq Haji Husein had a pro-western tendency and the president had chosen him in an attempt to improve relations with the West.

While its talks with Ethiopia did not yield any agreements, a meeting between President Adan Abdulle Osman and Jomo Kenyatta was in the offing. In an attempt to normalise its relations with Kenya, Somalia promised to disengage itself from the active pursuit of its irredentist goals. And as a goodwill gesture it expected Kenya to recognise its interest in the "welfare and destiny of the Somali people in Kenya".[168]

Acting upon Somalia's request, Nyerere set the stage for a meeting between President Kenyatta of Kenya and President Adan Abdulle Osman of Somalia — on the occasion of Tanzanian independence anniversary celebration. The meeting was to take place on 9 December in Arusha. However, a few days before the meeting, Kenyatta informed Nyerere that he would not be attending because of the preparation for Kenya's independence anniversary, scheduled for December 12. Instead, Kenyatta sent Joseph Murumbi, the foreign minister, and Mbiyu Konainge, minister of education, to meet the Somalis in Tanzania. After a brief meeting with Somali leaders, the two Kenyan ministers returned to Nairobi and persuaded President Kenyatta to go to Arusha and meet the Somali President. President Adan Abdulle Osman submitted a proposal which stated that, (i) the Somali government would stop any territorial claims, (ii) that Kenya would recognise Somalia's "interest in the welfare and destiny of the Somali people in Kenya", and (iii) that both sides would indicate willingness to reach a solution to the problem.[169]

The Somali proposal had two implications, the first was formulated as a face-saving formula and a deal as it promised to disengage itself from active pursuit of the territorial dispute. The second outcome could have been intended to gain a way to have a say in the affairs of the Somali people

---

168   Touval, 1972: 224.
169   *Ibid.*, 223-4.

in Kenya. However, Kenya feared that Somalia's initiative was a tactic to disrupt and alienate Ethiopia. Any deal which Somalia could have reached with one of the disputants separately could run the risk of being sabotaged by the other party. Kenya could not afford to lose Ethiopia's alliance in case of renewal of hostility with Somalia. To test Somalia's commitment to its proposal, Kenyatta asked Somalia to prove its sincerity by condemning the guerrilla activity, known as *shifta*, and to cease aiding it. Somalia rejected the proposals since Kenya accepted some similar proposal at the Rome talks in August 1963. During the Rome talks, in August 1963, Kenya suggested its position to recognise Somalia's interest in the future of Somalis residing in Kenya.[170]

Not only the Kenyan-Somali talks failed to bridge the gap between the two countries, instead they led to worsening of their relations. Consequently, guerrilla activities in Kenya intensified. And in reaction Kenya launched a diplomatic campaign accusing Somalia of adjust responsibility for the guerrilla activities. Despite the deterioration of relations, the Somali prime minister, Abdirisaq Haji Husein attended the Nairobi meeting of East and Central African states in March 1966.[171]

QUIET DIPLOMACY: THE PROCESS OF DISENGAGEMENT

On 10 June 1967, President Adan Abdulle Osman's six year term of office expired, and he lost the election to

---

170 *Ibid.*, 210-6.
171 *Ibid.*, 225.

Dr Abdirashiid Ali Sharmarke. On 20 July 1967, the new president appointed Mahamed Haji Ibrahim Egal as premier.

Rejecting the fruitless external policy of his predecessor, Premier Egal began pursuing a policy of detente by changing the aggressive political tone towards Somalia's neighbours to a more conciliatory one. He declared that Djibouti belonged to France and that the Djiboutians must negotiate with France for their independence. Then he met Kenyan and Ethiopian leaders at the October 1967 OAU meeting in Arusha, Tanzania, and exchanged positive views.

With the Kenyan representatives, Egal signed the Arusha Memorandum which stipulated normalising of relations and the ending of four year-old border dispute. In the same meeting the parties agreed to open more negotiations through the good offices of President Kenneth Kaunda of Zambia. This agreement also brought to an end the active period of Kenya's international diplomatic initiatives in its bid to counter the Somali claim. Later, at the end of 1967, Premier Egal re-established diplomatic relationship with Britain (which was cut in 1963).

Somalia's new foreign policy prompted US diplomats to support a wider economic community encompassing Kenya, Tanzania, Uganda, Ethiopia and Somalia which might provide a context in which "Somalis from all countries could have enhanced political freedom".[172] To commit itself further to this principle, Premier Egal began to stop the supply

---

172   Samatar et al, 1987: 139.

line of Somali guerrilla forces in Ethiopia and Kenya. He further ceased hostile propaganda against these countries. In spite of these new overtures by the Somali government, no progress was made on Somalia's application to the East African community

At home Prime Minister Egal's foreign policy of detente met stiff resistance. He was seen as drifting away from the Republic's foreign policy mainstream by normalising relations with the 'enemies' of the Somali nation. He was accused of a 'sell out'. In defence of his policy, Premier Egal said,

> "[...] What my government seeks to do is to foster an atmosphere of good will wherein it will be possible to negotiate at a round-table conference an equitable solution for the problems of these peoples without exposing them to the scourge of war. I am therefore surprised that there are elements who would like, for some other ulterior motives, to make people believe that there has been a compromise on principle and a sell-out at Kinshasa, Addis Ababa and Arusha. Is it a sell-out to persuade Kenya to leave the people of NFD in peace whilst still accepting to negotiate at the conference table the future of these people? Is it a sell-out to persuade Kenya to expose conditions in the area to the examination of a Three-State Working Committee?"[173]

---

173 Touval, 1972: 234.

Despite the revolt against Premier Egal's new policy, the Somali National Assembly approved the agreements reached by the Prime Minister by a majority of 89 to 1, with 4 abstentions. To give freedom of action and show the assembly's support, it also authorised the government to pursue the policy further and submit future agreement to the Assembly for approval.[174]

THE DISENGAGEMENT AND DETENTE

Towards the end of 1967 the relations between Somalia and its neighbours entered in a new stage. Before 1967 their inter-state relationship was going in a worsening direction; a hope of improvement in relations was seen impossible without solving the core issue of the dispute: the Somali territorial claims. As the issue was a "core value" associated with the "national-self", each side refused to accept anything less than a settlement of the dispute on its own terms.

The year 1967 is characterised by a change of approach in Somali policy. During this period a new government took office in Somalia which soon began to pursue a policy of detente. As a revisionist state, Somalia needed the other parties to negotiate. This new Somali government's initiative opened the gate for new agreements reached between Somalia and its disputing neighbours. The agreements changed the disputants inter-state relations from hostility to conciliation.

---

174 *Ibid.*, 239.

The detente became possible because of parties tacitly agreeing that their fundamental disagreement should not prevent the restoration of normal relations. Therefore, agreements reached had to be "formulated in a manner consistent with the position of each party on the principal issue in dispute"[175] and lent themselves to different interpretations. Each party was free to interpret the agreement as consistent with its "core value". Furthermore, parties developed an attitude to refrain from challenging the interpretations of the other side.

The breakthrough which marked the beginning of the negotiation came in September 1967, when Somalia and Kenya signed the Kinshasa Declaration during the 1967 Kinshasa OAU summit. With the help of President Kaunda, the two parties agreed to settle their dispute peacefully and to refrain from hostile propaganda. The agreement, also known as Joint Declaration, pledged both governments to "respect each other's sovereignty and territorial integrity".[176] To further extend their understanding, the two governments agreed to meet the following month.

On 28 October the parties met in Arusha. At the meeting Julius Nyerere and President Milton Obote of Uganda were also present. The Somali delegation was headed by the Prime Minster, Mahamed Haji Ibrahim Egal, while Kenyan delegation was led by President Kenyatta himself. The two governments reaffirmed their adherence to Kinshasa

---

175 *Ibid.*, 233
176 *Ibid.*, 230.

Declaration and pledged to normalise relations and to refrain from hostile propaganda against each other. They agreed to set a working-committee — Zambia would be a member — which would review the "implementation of the agreements, and examine ways and means of bringing about a satisfactory solution to major and minor differences between Kenya and Somalia".[177]

The Ethiopian-Somali negotiations also made some progress. In the previous three years, the disagreement over the venue of the talks between Ethiopia and Somalia hindered any serious negotiation between the two governments. Barely one week after the Kinshasa summit, Somalia and Ethiopia reached a series of agreements, in Addis Ababa, one of which reaffirmed the Khartoum and Accra agreements. They also decided to set a timetable for further periodic meetings.

To show its sincerity towards the agreements, Somalia halted *shifta* activity in both Ethiopia and Kenya, suspended the anti-Ethiopian and anti-Kenyan propaganda over its mass media, like Radio Muqdisho.

RELATIVE CALM

Somalia's interpretation of the agreements concluded was that it had major gains for its position. It believed that Kenya and Ethiopia accepted the existence of a dispute and "both have expressed willingness to try to find ways of solving it".[178]

---

177 *Ibid.*, 230-1.
178 *Ibid.*, 223.

It also claimed that both Kenya and Ethiopia had conceded Somalia to "have a say by way of consultation in the affairs and administration" of the NFD and Western Somaliland.[179] The Somali-French understanding of September 1968 was also to be interpreted as consistent with the principles of both parties. Somalia could point with satisfaction to the reference of "self-determination", and France to the phrase on "non-interference".[180]

However, Somalia's interpretation did not reflect the true facts of the agreements. It was more for local consumption and to give itself freedom of action. With the aim of softening people's perception about the government's handling of the territorial issues, the Somali government was set to create an atmosphere of willingness to negotiate with its rival parties.

For instance, the Kenya-Somali agreements in the Kinshasa Declaration stated merely that,

> "... both Governments have expressed their desire to respect each other's sovereignty and territorial integrity in the spirit of paragraph 3 of Article III of the OAU Charter".[181]

The Somali government defended that this phrase did give concessions since Somalia had already accepted this principle by its signature at the United Nations.

---

179 *Ibid.*, 234.
180 *Ibid.*, 235.
181 *Ibid.*, 234-5.

What caused the Somali government to pursue a policy of detente? After eight years — since independence in 1960 — of confrontation and hostility with its neighbours, the goal of putting all Somalis under a single state brought Somalia into diplomatic isolation. Ethiopia, Kenya and France had made no concessions. Any concession by these states would have impaired the integrity of their respective "national self".

The economic burden of the policy of confrontation also pressed heavily on Somalia. Furthermore, Ethiopia and Kenya's closure of their borders, had a tremendous impact on the pastoral economy, especially, the nomadic society who lived near these borders. Ethnic Somalis living in Ethiopia and Kenya suffered heavily because of the confrontation. Both Ethiopia and Kenya imposed emergency in these areas.

The closure of borders had also reduced drastically the trade between Somalia and its neighbours. The closure of the Suez canal in 1967, which had taken also economic toll on the other states of the Horn of Africa, made Somalia also feel the burden of continuation of confrontation and hostility.

The prospect which offered the disengagement was an inducement which pushed Somalia to follow a more pragmatic policy towards its neighbours. Somalia's neighbours responded favourably to the Somali initiatives, since they also stood to gain by disengagement. Both Ethiopia and Kenya felt the pinch of considerable military cost of the anti-*shifta* operations. On the other hand, both Ethiopia and Kenya hoped that this new diplomatic policy could make Somalia accept the *status quo* of the frontiers. In fact, they felt that the new policy could be the first stage towards this policy.

The success of the policy of the new Somali government lay in its ability to handle the case by using a "parallel" approach. This entailed making parallel progress with its adversaries simultaneously. Previously any negotiation by Somalia with its neighbours was futile. Ethiopia and Kenya suspected any negotiations reached separately with Somalia. For example, the 1965 Somali-Kenya negotiations in Arusha was torpedoed by Ethiopia which feared to lose Kenya's alliance. This was also to influence the Somali-French negotiations. Somali relations with France was a "necessary corollary of the Somali detente with Ethiopia".[182] As the disputes were interrelated, Somalia was prudent to make concurrent agreements with its neighbours. For example, the Kenya-Somali breakthrough of 1967 created a positive atmosphere for the forthcoming Somali-Ethiopian negotiations.

> Another major factor undoubtedly was the improvement of relations between Ethiopia and Kenya. The Somali hostility made them allies. It also made for peaceful end to the territorial dispute between Ethiopia and Kenya. In fact, Kenya government which was concerned with the threat from Somalia, agreed to give up the control of Gadaduma wells to Ethiopia. In previous years Gadaduma was their main meat of the dispute. In exchange, Ethiopia recognised Kenya's possession of the Gadaduma

---

182 *Ibid.*, 243.

wells.[183] It was these negotiations which prepared the ground for Ethiopia and Kenya to set up a military alliance.

EXTERNAL FACTORS

Many factors combined to induce and facilitate the process of disengagement and detente. One of these factor was the spirit of pan-African solidarity as it was used to justify the commitment to disengagement and detente. Although the OAU's role was limited, it provided an opportunity for the parties to meet. For example, the opening breakthrough of the negotiations between the disputants took place in September 1967 OAU summit in Kinshasa. On the other hand, any major agreement reached by the disputants at the OAU summit conferences "endowed the declaration with its own prestige"; it made the document an official OAU document.[184]

The policies of the major powers had also played a role in shaping the detente. Both the United States and Britain encouraged the detente. Both states hoped the detente might diminish the Soviet influence in the Horn.

The Soviet Union which was in the process of extending its influence in Africa, also seemed to have favoured a detente. In spite of the Soviet alliance with Somalia, it did not want to be identified with one side — least with Somalia. All these factors made the detente possible. Touval explained that,

---

183   *Ibid.*, 247-8.
184   *Ibid.*, 242.

"the complementary perceptions by the parties of the circumstances and options faced by them, and the willingness and ability to take reciprocal steps toward their common goal of disengagement, resulted in a detente".[185]

UNSTABLE DETENTE

In spite of this commitment, the detente remained highly unstable. Many factors were thwarting this trend: (i) the contentious issue of the territorial dispute between the parties was considered "core value" associated with the "national-self" and so no party could afford to give up its claim — such claims led to no-compromise, (ii) Somalia never renounced its irredentist objectives, and (iii) before any progress could be reached on the 1967-68 agreements, both Ethiopia and Somalia political landscapes changed following the military coups which occurred in both countries between 1969 to 1972.

The military government of General Mahamed Siyad Barre which took power in October 1969, assured Ethiopia and Kenya that it would continue its predecessor's policy.[186] Siyad Barre's military government from 1969 to 1974 may be characterised as a period of concentration on internal problems. This entailed mainly consolidation of his regime and

---

185   Ibid., 245.
186   Touval, 1972: 245.

institutionalisation of the October revolution.[187] However, it was the second stage when the military government undertook a vast international campaign to denounce what it dubbed as "the colonial" behaviour of Ethiopia towards the Somalis in Western Somaliland.

Under the auspices of the OAU, a new dialogue was started between Somalia and Ethiopia in 1971, but at the end of 1972 the two parties' positions were so far apart that negotiations failed. Ethiopia reinforced its military presence along the border with Somalia. Kenya did the same. Feeling the threat, Somalia took the matter to the OAU.

TABLE 1: CHRONOLOGICAL SUMMARY OF 1967-8 SOMALI- ETHIOPIAN - KENYAN NEGOTIATIONS

October 26, 1967	Somalia and Ethiopia exchanged seized aircraft, in accordance with September agreements reached in Addis Ababa.
November 23-30, 1967	Somali-Ethiopian negotiations at ambassadorial level take place in Addis Ababa on the implementation of the September agreements.
December 1, 1967	Talks take place "at summit" on the occasion of ceremonies inaugurating the East African Economic Community in Arusha. Present (among others): Emperor Haile Selassie, Presidents Kaunda, Kenyatta, Shermarke.

---

187   Samatar et al, 1987: 141.

December 15-16, 1967	Talks take place in East and Central African Summit Conference, Kampala. Present (amount other): Emperor Haile Selassie, Presidents Kaunda, Kenyatta, Prime Minster Egal. Kenya and Somalia reach an agreement on the terms of reference of the working committee decided upon at Arusha. Somalia formally applies for member in the East African Economic Community.
January 27, 1968	Kenyan ministerial delegation visits Mogadishu. Subsequently announcement on the establishment of diplomatic relations and the lifting of trade embargoes.
February 5-8, 1968	Ethiopian Foreign Minster's visits Mogadishu. Progress on the implementation of the agreement reached in Addis Ababa in September.
July 4-28, 1968	President Shermarke and Prime Minster Egal on an official visit to Kenya (Kaunda not present). Agree to convene the working committee, decided upon in Arusha in October, "soon".
August 30, 1968	Conclusion of Kenyan-Somali talks in Kismayu. At the administrative level, they deal with security along the border, land communication and trade. (This was not the working committed of Kenyan, Somali, and Zambian representatives mentioned above).
	Communiqué emphasizes that the talks were of an exploratory nature, aimed at the eventual settlement of major issue (italics added).
September 5-6 1968	Parties meet again at the OAU summit at Algiers. Apparently, no substantive negotiations on Somali dispute as participants with other issues, notable the Biafra-Nigerian conflict.

September 20-21, 1968	Prime Minister Egal visits Paris to talks with President de Gaulle. Communiqué: Egal explained his policy of détente toward all neighbouring countries; both governments stated that they are inspired by the same principle — respect for independence, the right of all peoples to self-determination through democratic procedure and without foreign interference, non-interference by any state in the internal affairs of others — and agreed on good neighbour policy; France stated that it would examine sympathetically Somali suggestions for French co-operation in Somalia's development (i.e. Somali requests for aid).
February 21, 1969	Prime Minister Egal and President Kenyatta hold talk in Nairobi, with President Kaunda present. Communiqué: satisfaction expressed at progress in normalization of relations; Kenya agreed to grant an amnesty to political offenders who fled the country and to lift the state of emergency in the Northeastern Province; both sides will ease restriction on the movement of livestock across the border; will co-operate in improving communications and in joint development projects; will discuss further relaxation of currency exchange restrictions.
March 15, 1969	Emergency regulations lifted in Kenya's Northeastern Province.

Source: Touval, 1972: 231-33

CHAPTER SIX

THE IMPACT OF THE COLD WAR IN THE HORN

Covering three quarters of a million square miles of land, the Horn of Africa is the eastern-most tip of the African continent. Geographically, it is formed by two prominent landmarks: the East African highlands and the Nile basin, which also represent social and cultural watersheds separating the peoples of the Horn from those in adjacent regions.[188] The Horn conventionally comprises Ethiopia, Eritrea, Somalia and Djibouti (and the Sudan which is also considered as a central African country).

Situated near the vital tri-junction of the three continents of Africa, Asia and Europe, the Horn is a region of great

---

188 Markakis, 1990: 3.

strategic importance and is a hotbed of conflicting interests both internal and external. To protect their respective national interests, the rival countries of the Horn have been leaning towards external help which in turn has created a situation where external powers can interfere.

In spite of the fact that the international involvement in the Horn region came into focus in the wake of the 1977-8 conflict, it actually predates the recent conflict by a century. For hundreds of years, since the time of Vasco de Gama's visit to India in the fifteenth century, the Horn of Africa has commanded a strategic significance. The Horn continued to gain importance through the following three centuries. With the emergence of the Nile valley diplomacy in the middle of the nineteenth century, the region began to gain strategic importance as it commanded a considerable part of the head-waters of the Nile, and provided from the East the most direct access route to the Nile valley.[189] With the rise of Egypt, the Nile and the Nile valley gained strategic importance within the orbit of the policy framework of Britain and France. This political set-up later led to the Abyssinians (present Ethiopia), who sit at one the water-heads of the Nile, dominating European policy regarding Africa.

The strategic importance of the Horn has been highlighted by the region's proximity to the Middle East and the Gulf's oil-fields and the Indian Ocean trade routes which became more important in recent years. The West

---

189   Bhardwaj, 1979: 24.

has a vital interest in keeping open Bab-el-Mandeb, the port of Djibouti and the Red Sea for its international shipping. Bab-el-Mandeb which narrows the Arabian Peninsula and the African coast to only 22 miles apart, is where the Red Sea and the Indian Ocean meet through the Gulf of Aden. Farther down the strait near Perim island, the narrow strait, the navigable area is reduced to only 16 miles. This made the strait a crucial place. Whichever superpower controlled this region could have advantage over the other.

The increasing superpower interest in the Red Sea and the Horn area during the reopening of the Suez canal in June 1975 transformed the Red Sea from an "appendix of the Indian Ocean into a major artery",[190] in terms of economic and strategic importance, connecting the Indian Ocean and the Mediterranean. This development reflected the strategic importance which the Indian Ocean attained in the context of the world-wide balance of power between the West and the East.

The British occupation of Aden in 1839 enabled Britain to control the strait along the flow of Red Sea traffic through the Suez Canal. Following Britain's decline in the 1960s, the US, who already had bases in Eritrea, filled the gap. This made it possible for Washington to control the southern approach of the Red sea, while the Soviet Union, who allied with the pro-Soviet Egypt, controlled the northern approach. The withdrawal of the British

---

190 *Ibid.*, 18-9.

from Aden, increasing Egyptian dependence on Russia and the installation of a pro-Moscow radical Gaffar Al Nimery in Sudan contributed to the rise of the Russian influence in the Horn.[191]

Following the Arab-Israeli conflict of 1967, which led to the Suez closure, the US began to lose interest in Bab-el-Mandeb's strategic significance and the surrounding area of the Red Sea. The Soviet Union began to increase its influence in the region when it made footholds in Somalia, South Yemen and Sudan. This helped the Russians to gain control of the southernmost approach to the Red Sea.

THE SUPERPOWERS IN THE HORN OF AFRICA

As colonies became independent, the mode of competition changed to influencing countries indirectly rather than establishing direct control as was the case in the colonial era.[192] During the Cold War, the Horn of Africa's strategic location near the oil-rich Middle East was of great value to the superpowers. To further their strategic interests, both the former Soviet Union and the United States took advantage of the opportunity of the Somali-- Ethiopian dispute, heightening the volatile relationships of the Horn of Africa states in the 1970s and early 1980s. The resulting rivalry created a situation whereby the superpowers to pour substantial economic

---

191   *Ibid.*, 132.
192   Issa-Salwe, 1996: 78-95.

and military assistance into this region. Since the twentieth century, this part of the world has rarely witnessed peace, until new boundaries appeared — witnessing the birth of the Eritrean Republic in 1992. This new development made the Red Sea area an 'Arab lake'.

The internal conflict in the Horn of Africa tempted the external powers to interfere. The US, the Soviet Union, some European and Middle Eastern countries such as Britain, Italy, France, Saudi Arabia, Iran, Iraq and Egypt have been providing arms and other forms of aid to this region. To safeguard their respective national interests, the rival countries in the Horn of Africa have been leaning on outside help. The realignment of the national interest of the Horn states showed that ideology was not relevant. Ideology, like religion, "has been used as a public relations cover".[193] For example, communist China was aligned with the capitalist West against Russia.

Ever since the Tsarist times, Russia has been looking to establish a sea route between its western and eastern ports through Bab-el-Mandeb at the entrance of the Red Sea and the Suez. In 1950s the USSR established relations with Egypt. However, things changed by 1972 when its relations with Egypt went sour as Anwar Sadat began a policy targeted to gain economic and military support from the United States.[194] Already a few years before this period the Soviet Union had established a

---

193 Bhardwaj, 1979: 139.
194 Makinda, 1993: 51-2.

foothold in the Horn. While its relation with Egypt was waning, the Soviet Union's relation with Somalia was taking the opposite direction. In July 1974, the Soviet Union forged a close military alliance with Somalia, and signed a Treaty of Friendship and Co-operation. The treaty included protection as well as both military and economic assistance for Somalia. At Berbera on the Red Sea, they built a dry dock, missile handling and storage facilities, a communication station, large fuel facilities, and a 15,000 foot runway capable of accommodating large Soviet aircraft.[195] In Armis, near Muqdisho, they also built a giant radar and other communication receiver facilities and transmitter sites.[196] At Kismaayo, in the southern part of the country, they had a large communication centre.

Until 1970, the Horn of Africa occupied a minor place in the United States' strategy, for it could play little role in promoting the American interest in the Indian Ocean zone between 1960 and 1970. During this period, Washington focused its attention on the establishment of military bases along the Soviet border, such as the Iran-Pakistan-Turkey northern tier.[197] These bases were to serve the US as launching pads for nuclear attacks on the Soviet targets in the event of war.

The US established a military presence in the Horn in the 1950s, when it built a military communication

---

195   *Ibid.*, 52.
196   Issa-Salwe, 1996: 86.
197   Bhardwaj, 1979: 143.

base at Kagnew in Eritrea (then a province of Ethiopia. Eritrea is now an independent state). Kagnew provided US military and NATO world-wide communications network. Following the improvements in satellite technology in the early 1970s the US interest in Kagnew decreased.

Following the development of the Inter-Continental Ballistic Missile (ICBM), the tier bases of Iran-Pakistan-Turkey strategy was greatly reduced. However, following the energy crisis in 1970s Washington's interests changed in this part of the world as this gave rise to a new concept of the US and Western security interests based "on commercial and economic rather that the old type of geo-strategic needs".[198]

The Soviet naval base at Berbera, was considered by the United States and its allies as a threat to vital western security interests in the Gulf and Indian Ocean regions. To counter this the US administration began to fund the expansion of naval facilities on the Indian Ocean island of Diego Garcia (leased by Britain in 1965). The Diego Garcia base was a few thousand nautical miles nearer to the Gulf region than Kagnew.

In promoting its economic interest and to counter the Soviet threat, during this period the Americans established an alliance with the regional powers constituting the Saudi Arabia-Egypt-Sudan alliance. Financed by Saudi Arabia and cemented by mutual defence pacts, this Afro-Arab

---

198   *Ibid.*, 143-4.

alliance became an important factor in Africa as it was also to serve the US and Western interest without being exposed to the charge of openly interfering in Africa.[199]

THE HORN CONFLICT: INSTABILITY IN THE ETHIOPIAN POLITICAL ESTABLISHMENT

Meanwhile, in early 1974, a new political threat was looming on the horizon of Ethiopia as Emperor Haile Selassie's feudal monarchy was crippled by waves of demonstrations organised by the Ethiopian People's Revolutionary Party (EPRP), the Ethiopian Democratic Union (EDU), students, teachers and workers' groups. Haile Selassie sent his troops to quell the demonstrations. This caused more resentment. Soon the situation got out of hand. On 12 September, 1974 the Ethiopian army took advantage of the deteriorating circumstances and deposed the Emperor, who had ruled Ethiopia for four decades.[200]

With the change in government came a change in political ideology. The Soviet Union who was monitoring the situation, found a breeding ground for its ideology with the military regime which showed communist tendencies. In view of the new political atmosphere in the region, the Soviet strategists sensed a new opportunity: to expand Soviet influence by creating a Pax-Sovietica federation based on Marxist-Leninist ideology among Somalia, Ethiopia

---

199   *Ibid.*, 145-7.
200   Issa-Salwe, 1996: 82

and the People's Democratic Republic of Yemen. In March 1976 Castro began to implement this plan by paying official visits to the region. And Soviet President Podgorny visited the following month to promote the idea.[201] However, the plan failed when Somalia insisted that the Western Somaliland issue be solved before any confederation was created.

Meanwhile, in Ethiopia the political situation was worsening as General Aman Andom, the chairman of the Dergue (the Ethiopian Revolutionary Government) was killed, along with some 60 high ranking officials, and replaced by General Tafari Banti. After a short time, a group led by Lieutenant-Colonel Mengistu Haile Mariam eliminated General Tafari Banti and took power.

The new military government which showed socialist tendencies soon scrapped the United States military communication base which was established in the 1950s. These new events induced the USSR to consolidate its presence in the Horn, an area previously dominated by the United States and its allies. In 1977 the United States pulled out of Ethiopia, and its place was taken by the Soviet Union, thus marking a turning point in superpower relations with the Horn.

---

201   Markakis, 1990: 229.

The Ethiopian-Somali War

The political turmoil in Ethiopia gave Somalia a chance to retake the missing territory. In June 1977, the Somali government decided to commit its army to the liberation of Western Somaliland and to help the Western Somali Liberation Front (WSLF) which had increased its operations since the beginning of the 1970s. Backed by the Somali army, WSLF launched a massive offensive and liberated nearly all the Somali-inhabited Western Somaliland within a short time by capturing main towns such as Jigjiga, Goday (Gode), Dhagahbuur, and, very briefly, Dire Dawa.

Menaced internally as well as externally, the military regime in Addis Ababa declared itself a Marxist-Leninist state, and appealed to the Soviet Union for military assistance. As a result, the Soviet Union shifted its alliance from Somalia to Ethiopia by moving its military advisers from Muqdisho and flying them directly to Addis Ababa. It announced in October 1977 that they would stop the arms supply to Somalia and that it had decided to help Ethiopia repulse the Somali attack. Other than strategic reasons, Soviet decision was also based on the assumption that Ethiopian society was going through a social revolution that "held promise of socialism taking root"[202]

In reaction to the Soviet decision, on 13 November, 1977 Somalia abrogated the 10 year Treaty of Friendship

---

202 Ibid., 229.

and Co-operation signed in 1974, and ordered all Soviet advisors to leave the country within 17 days. Somalia turned to the West and to the moderate Arab countries for military and financial help.

China welcomed Somalia's break with Moscow, but turned down Siyad Barre's appeal for military assistance. China which strongly objected to the Soviet-Cuban intervention in the Horn, avoided becoming militarily involved. Instead, it opted to encourage Africans to reject the threat of 'Soviet imperialism'.

The Ethiopian Dergue claimed that Somalia committed 70,000 troops, 600 tanks, 600 artillery pieces and 40 fighter planes in the war.[203] However, by April 1978 the situation began to change drastically in favour of the Dergue, as the help which Somalia expected from the Western powers and the Arab League countries failed to materialise. The war then stalled in the Ogaden thus giving the Soviets time between October 1977 and February 1978 to deliver substantial quantities of war material, trained combatants and technicians to Ethiopia.[204] In the meantime, the Soviet Union had reinforced the Ethiopian army with 18,000 Cuban soldiers, along with Yemeni and East German technicians. The Ethiopian's stunning victory could not have come about without Moscow's massive airlift of arms, which included 400 tanks, 200 other armoured vehicles,

---

203   Bhardwaj, 1979: 117.
204   Legum et al, 1979: 7.

300 heavy guns, about 75 modern MIG fighter bombers, and 200 military helicopters.[205]

The Somali invasion of Ethiopia proved a miscalculation. On the contrary it created a favourable atmosphere for the new Ethiopian regime, which faced a strong internal dissent. It, in fact, became a patriotic political propaganda which the Dergue dexterously used to weld public support. This resulted also in a disadvantageous situation for opponents of the military regime.

INTERNATIONAL DIMENSIONS OF THE HORN CONFLICT

The opening of the Suez Canal in 1869 created a geopolitical situation which increased the competition for control of the coast along the Red Sea and the Indian Ocean among the European colonial powers. On the other hand, Suez canal decreased the importance of the Cape route.

External intervention played a major role in determining the emergent pattern of political forces and the balance of power in Africa after independence. The Soviet-Cuban intervention in Angola and Ethiopian-Somali conflict, France and Belgium's intervention in the internal affairs of their former colonies are a few examples. Intervention was also decisive in shaping the emergent pattern of political forces and the balance of power in the Horn in the period between 1977 and 1978. The Somali Republic, whose

---

205   Bhardwaj, 1979: 118.

allies failed to match the military assistance received by the Dergue, was the main loser.

According to US intelligence by early February 1978, the Soviet Union became active in Eritrea struggle.[206] Eritrea and its ports of Assab and Massawa were important for Russia, for they commanded entrance to the Red Sea. However, the Russians were never interested in Ethiopia's victory over Eritrea, for it would have made them redundant in Ethiopia. Ironically, Russia had helped Eritrean liberation movements in the early sixties against the feudal government of Haile Selassie.

In the summer of 1977, the long-standing territorial dispute in the Horn of Africa was complicated by a dramatic switch in alliance of the Somalis and Ethiopians. The Dergue which showed extremist leftist sympathy broke with the West, while Somalia, by ending the Black Africa's first friendship and co-operation with Moscow, turned to the United States. Both countries decided to break with the past before securing alternative support. In early 1978 when the Soviet Union decided to intervene in the Western Somaliland war, Soviet-American relations were in "a state of uncertainty and flux".[207]

---

206 Legum et al, 1979: 15.
207 Brzezinski, 1983: 205.

THE SOVIET-CUBAN MILITARY INVOLVEMENT IN THE HORN

The Soviet and its allies' help to Ethiopia in the Ogaden war was seen as legitimate in resisting the aggression of one of OAU member-states against another. Somalia was considered to be an aggressor trying to impose its territorial boundary on Ethiopia by force. However, the legitimisation of the external involvement had another implication for the African states. As enshrined in the OAU Charter, the avowed philosophy of African independence is that African conflicts should be resolved by Africans themselves. Africa's weakness created a vacuum which non-African powers could easily fill. The political and economic weakness made many African countries align themselves with one block or the other.

The West's attempt to counter Soviet influence in the Red Sea was frustrated by its irreconcilability with Somali irredentist ambitions. Endorsing Somali aims would have not only antagonised Ethiopia and Kenya, but also contravened one of OAU's fundamental principles. The outcome enabled the Soviet Union and Cuba to partially succeed in establishing a strong initiative in the Horn and strengthened their position across the sea in South Yemen, with its port of Aden. The Soviet leadership was thus able to take on the West in a situation where the West had no chance to respond without taking the undesirable step of linking Soviet behaviour in Africa to sensitive East-West issues elsewhere.

Despite the fact that Western countries objected to the foreign involvement in the Ogaden conflict, they were also unanimous in upholding the OAU position. As a result of this view, the West refused to assist Muqdisho militarily. This left Somalia with the support of a mainly Islamic coalition of regional powers, some of which had military ties with the East (Syria and Iraq) and others with the West (Egypt, Saudi Arabia, Iran and the Sudan). Although, the agreements under which these countries obtained arms from Washington and Moscow prohibited them from passing them on to third parties, they did not prevent some countries, like Iraq and Pakistan, from giving Somalia some military equipment.

In 1964 during a border clash between Somalia and Ethiopia, the Third Division of the Ethiopian army was already on its way to Hargeysa, the North-Western capital region of Somalia, when the Ethiopian government decided not to invade Somalia. In 1978, shortly before the defeat of the Somali army, the possibility of an Ethiopian invasion of Somalia once again surfaced. To avoid this the United States pressed the Soviet Union to restrain the Ethiopian army and prevent them from crossing their "recognised border". To be ready for such eventuality, however Egypt, in collaboration with the United States, put some of its forces in Somalia.[208] Iran and Saudi Arabia would also send their troops into the Horn in defence of the Somalis.[209]

---

208   Ibid., 181.
209   Bhardwaj, 1979: 118.

While the West and the Somalia's Arab allies refused to help Somalia, both accepted that if this fear became a reality, Muqdisho would be entitled to military support to protect its sovereignty.

During the war, the US agreed to provide Somalia with defensive and economic aid, provided that Somalia withdraw from the Ogaden. Somalia ordered its forces to withdraw on 10 March. However, once Somali troops did withdraw, the State Department withheld virtually all military material promised by the Carter administration.

The Carter administration had hardly entered office when the first hostilities began. Its first year was spent trying to find a coherent policy vis-a-vis the Soviet Union to make progress on issues such as arms negotiations, the European balance, the Middle East, and "an appropriate mix of co-operation and conflict".[210]

In May 1977, just after the Ethiopian military junta broke with the US, the USSR and Ethiopia entered a secret arms agreement in Moscow. Some sources estimated that over $1 billion worth of Soviet military was given to Ethiopia over the following 12 months. Moscow's massive airlift began in late September 1977, shipping through Aden. By early February 1978, Western intelligence sources put the number of Russian advisers at 1,000 and Cubans at 3,000.[211] This was comparable roughly in volume to

---

210 *Ibid.*, 205.
211 Legum et al, 1979: 13-4.

the arms shipped to the MPLA (Movemento Popular de Libertacao de Angola) during the Angolan conflict.[212] The Soviets provided Ethiopia with 18,000 Cuban troops and Soviet experts to help with the Ethiopian war effort. To make sure that the war was won, they sent General Vasely Petrov, the first Deputy Commander-in- Chief of the Soviet ground operations, and General Arnaldo Ochoa, a Cuban general who was engaged in Angola in 1976.[213]

Shortly after the Americans pulled out of Ethiopia, the Carter administration started sending contradictory signals to Somalia. To woo Somalia into switching from the Soviet sphere, in 1975 Saudi Arabia offered to take over economic aid projects then financed by Moscow, and to buy US arms for Somalia in order to replace the Soviet weapons.[214] In obscure circumstances, however, the then US Secretary of State, Henry Kissinger, objected to the Saudi Arabian idea. The possible reason for Kissinger's opposition to Somalia switching to the western camp was that if the Soviets were expelled from Somalia at that time, it would be difficult for the United States administration to convince Congress to approve funds for the expansion of Diego Garcia facilities.

On 10 June 1977 Jimmy Carter insisted that the US would challenge the Soviet Union aggressively in many

---

212 Porter, 1984: 83-200.
213 Legum et al, 1979: 14; Brzezinski, 1983: 205
214 Makinda, 1993: 52-3.

areas of the world.[215] He mentioned the Horn of Africa, especially Somalia, as one of the areas in which the US wanted to challenge the Soviet presence. On 1 July Cyrus Vance, the US Secretary of State, also expressed similar concern about the Soviet presence in the Horn. In the following week, he disclosed that the Carter administration was ready to furnish Somalia with some defensive arms "in conjunction with a number of other countries".[216] However, the US government was cautious of not igniting sensitive issues such as that of boundaries or territorial questions. Basically the boundary issues were considered as a serious threat to the existence of many states in Africa. Many African states were vulnerable and suspicious of any challenge to the colonial defined boundaries, fearing that the framework of existing political equation in the continent might be swept away in an anarchy of nationalism and other conflicts. Somalia, in the eyes of many African countries, was considered to be the aggressor trying to impose its territorial boundary on Ethiopia by force. Against this political background, in August 1977 the United States decided not to give Somalia arms.[217]

However, following the Iranian revolution and the Soviet intervention in Afghanistan, the Carter administration signed agreements with Somalia, Kenya and Sudan to gain access to their military facilities. The agreement

---

215 Ibid., 54.
216 *Ibid.*, 54-5.
217 Issa-Salwe, 199: 88.

allowed the United States to use the former Soviet base at Berbera for what was to become the newly formed Rapid Development Task Force in 1980s.

WESTERN REACTION

Throughout the development of the Horn crisis, Washington made little effort to counter Soviet intervention in the Western Somaliland war. The Soviet propaganda portrayed the war in the Horn as entirely the policy of NATO powers in wishing to establish a 'Red Sea bloc' to perpetuate the split between the Arab and non-Arab states of the region and to gain control over the countries bordering the Red Sea.

TABLE 2: SOVIET WEAPONS SHIPMENTS TO ETHIOPIA DURING THE OGADEN WAR, MARCH 1977- MAY 1978

Types of weapons	Number transferred
T-34 tanks	30-56
T-54/55 tanks T-62 tanks	300-400 A few 200-300
Other armoured vehicle, including BTR-152 APCs	40
BMP-1 AFVs	Some
MiG-17s	Some 55-60
MiG-21s	12-20
MiG-23s	Some A few 30

Mi-4 helicopters	Several hundred
Mi-6 heavy transport helicopters	Thousands (?)
Mi-8 helicopters	Some
SAM-7 missiles	At least 28 launchers
	Over 300
Sagger anti-tank missiles	
SAM-3 missiles	Some Six
BM-21 rocket launchers	Numerous
	Thousands
Artillery guns, 100mm to 152mm	
Artillery guns, 152mm to 185mm	
Mobile anti-aircraft guns, 57mm Mortars	
Small arms	

Source: Porter,1984:200.

The West in turn was anxious to counter Russian influence in order to prevent it from getting access to the regional resources such as oil. Particularly, the US feared that the Russian entrenchment in the region would liquidate the private American interest in the area through radical socio-economic programmes in the littoral countries of the Horn.

The Americans advocated the idea that African problems should be left to the OAU. America's appeal suggested that the US was less able to manipulate the course of African policy. On the other hand, this policy was undermined by the OAU's inability to overcome internal differences. Nevertheless, this did not mean that Washington neglected its economic or strategic interests. To protect its strategic interests, the US kept a watch on the developing situation in the Horn. The West was deeply concerned over the communist challenge to the oil economic sea routes.

While Russia is almost self-sufficient in its energy requirements, the West, particularly Europe and Japan, has to depend completely on oil from this area.[218] The West, therefore, welcomed the US presence in the region as a deterrent against any disruption of the vital sea lanes.

On 12 January 1978, President Carter announced that the US would use its ability to bring peace into the Horn disputes without involving itself into "disputes that could be resolved by Africans themselves".[219] Yet the US could not remain passive while the Soviet bloc was involved in "changing the regional power to suit its own interest". Washington worried that if the Soviet-sponsored Cubans determined the outcome of an Ethiopian-Somali conflict, there could be wider regional and international consequences which could undermine United States credibility in the region.[220] The new political climate caused a concern to the regional powers, namely Egypt, Saudi Arabia and *Iran*.

On 11 February 1978, Cyrus Vance, the US Secretary of State, asked Moscow to withdraw their forces and those of the Cubans from Ethiopia. The obtrusive Soviet disinclination to reduce the Soviet-Cuban military forces was seen in Washington as a possible threat to detente. The US warned that the continuing Russian military involvement in the Horn could hamper progress in the vital Strategic Arms Limitation Talks (SALT). On 27 February 1978, the first

---

218 Bhardwaj, 1979: 137-8.
219 Legum et al, 1979: 11.
220 Brzezinski, 1983: 183.

diplomatic salvo which was to link the Horn conflict with the superpower nuclear limitation talks was fired by Carter's national security adviser, Zbigniew Brzezinski when he warned of the possibility of Soviet policy in the Horn prejudicing the SALT talks. He said that the "SALT lies buried in the sands of the Ogaden".[221] The US faced enigma of linking the Ogaden issue with SALT.

While the United States and its allies anxiously continued to debate how to deal with Russian threat in Africa, the Russians continued to hold the initiatives. The gap developed due to these strains was reflected in Carter's speech of 8 June 1978 when he declared that disputes or threats to peace would complicate the quest for a successful agreement on SALT. He said that, "This is not a matter of our preference, but a simple recognition of facts. The Soviets Union can choose either confrontation or co-operation.".[222]

THE US DILEMMA: REGIONALIST VS GLOBALIST APPROACH

Washington faced a political dilemma on how to respond to the 'Russian threats in Africa'. Inside the inner circles of Carter's administration there appeared to have developed regionalist and globalist groups. Championed by Cyrus Vance, the regionalists' (or softline) approach urged that the problems should be left to the OAU to handle. This policy

---

221   Ibid., 186.
222   Legume et al, 1979: 12.

cautioned the United States not to be identified with the aggressor (Somalia in this case). Otherwise this could lead to the wrong side of one of Africa's most cherished principles — the territorial integrity of the post-colonial states.

Countering with a globalist perspective (or hardline approach) Brzezinski urged that the US had to challenge the Soviet power wherever it emerged in the world. While he believed that the regional powers had to be motivated by their own self-interest to reject Soviet-Cuban involvement, it was the responsibility of the United States to give them confidence. If the United States failed to counter the Soviet menace, he reiterated, it could give green light to the Soviets to challenge Western interest in the future. To counter this menace, Brzezinski maintained, Washington should supply Somalia with arms equivalent to those provided to Ethiopia by the Soviets.[223] To send a strong message to the Soviet Union, he further advocated that the United States should deploy an American aircraft task force near the Horn.[224] He warned that the perceived US passivity in this strategic area would have not only foreign implications, but it would have domestic impact well. Brzezinski concluded that the signing of SALT would coincide with the time the Soviet-Cuban offensive takes place.

Siyad Barre who had previously tried to use foreign allies for his perceived interest, tried to strengthen the globalist position by urging the United States to assume its proper

---

223 *Ibid.*, 183; Samatar et al, 1987: 143.
224 Brzezinski, 1983: 182.

role in world affairs.[225] However, it was the intervention of Andrew Young, Carter's UN ambassador — himself an ardent supporter of the regionalist approach — which made the Vance position win out.

NATO analysts displayed considerable concern about the lack of political will shown by their governments in the face of Russian challenge. NATO military analysts believed that the Soviet Union was pursuing long-term aims in Africa, one of which was to establish military bases from where it could control the oil routes out of the Gulf, Saudi Arabia and Iran.[226] According to the analysts, the Russians had already a floating dry-dock moved from Berbera to an island near Massawa (in present Eritrea) which could enable them to control the southern entrance to the Red Sea leading to the Suez Canal.[227]

The competition for control of Horn and the importance of the Bab-el-Mandeb and the Red Sea were also to become Israel's concern. Israel feared the Arabisation of the Red Sea. To counter such development and to secure the Red Coast and find a passage along the Red Sea for its shipping and its oil supply from the Gulf, Israel formed close relationships with the only non-Arab littoral state, the Marxist Ethiopia despite the diverse political complexions of the two countries.

---

225 Samatar et al., 1987: 143.
226 Brzezinski, 1983: 183.
227 Legum et al,1979:12.

During the Somali-Ethiopian war in 1978, Moshe Dayan, the Israeli Defence Minister, admitted that Israel gave Ethiopia military and technical assistance.[228] To further the Ethiopian interest, it is believed that, the American Jewish lobby campaigned against the provision of US arms to Somalia during the Ogaden conflict in 1977-1978.

To undermine Ethiopia's close link with Israel, the Arab states supported Somalia and the Eritrean independence movement. What all these developments showed was that the conflict of the Horn became an extension of the Arab-Israeli conflict.

According to US intelligence the Soviet activity was not confined only to the campaign in the Ogaden. By early February 1978, it was believed that they were also active in Eritrea.[229] Eritrea and its ports of Assab and Massawa were important for Russia, for they commanded entrance to the Red Sea. However, the Russians were never interested in Ethiopia's victory over Eritrea, for it would have made them reduntant in Ethiopia. Ironically, Russia had helped Eritrean liberation movements in the early sixties against the feudal government of Haile Selassie.

---

228 Bhardwaj, 1979: 148.
229 Legum et al, 1979: 15

Chapter Seven
THE IMPACT OF THE END OF THE COLD WAR IN THE HORN

Geopolitically, the superpowers withdrawal from the Horn in the period 1989-1990 led to the marginalisation of African affairs, which were already on the "periphery of world politics".[230] The end of the Cold War made redundant — perhaps for the time being — the strategic value which the Horn had assumed during the Cold War.

THE IMPACT OF SOMALIA'S IRREDENTIST POLICIES

Article IV paragraph 4 of Somali Constitution of 1961 emphasised that "the Somali Republic promotes by legal and

---

230   Makinda, 1993: 89.

peaceful means, the union of Somali territories"[231] and that all ethnic Somalis, no matter where they reside, were citizens of the Republic. To progress towards its goal through these means Somalia pursued every diplomatic effort it could in order to bring its dispute to the world's attention. However, the exhausting battles for Western Somaliland and the NFD during the 1960s brought Somalia only diplomatic isolation. Amid the height of hostility with Ethiopia in 1964, Somalia sought remedy from the OAU. At an emergency council of ministers in Dar-es-Salaam, the OAU passed a resolution calling for respect and acceptance of colonial inherited boundaries. In reaction, the Somali National Assembly unanimously passed its own resolution declaring that the OAU stance "should not bind the Somali Government".[232]

Somalia's attempt to put its kinsmen under the Somali nation-state led the republic to detach itself from the common spirit of its sister states, and the goal looked more remote than ever. Somalia's policy with respect to the territories claimed had not yielded any fruit, and its cause had made no progress. Ethiopia, Kenya, and France had made no concessions and Somalia's irredentism had not elicited political support from other states.

By the end of 1963, the Somali leadership was weary of trying to find a diplomatic solution to its territorial claims. At home it faced growing opposition because of its lack of achievement. The failure to realise concrete results

---

231   Somali Constitution, 1961
232   Samatar et al, 1987: 138.

through diplomacy, and its irredentist policy which caused the victimisation and marginalisation of ethnic Somalis in Ethiopia, Kenya and French Somaliland contributed to the hostile attitude towards Western countries. In fact, in November 1963, the Prime Minister, Dr Sharmarke, announced the Republic's refusal of western military assistance in favour of Russian military aid amounting to nearly $22 million. Furthermore, breaking off diplomatic relations with Britain in 1963, Somalia not only lost British aid, which amounted to £1.3 million per year, but also an important diplomatic leverage.[233]

Soon after national independence, Somalia began to seek aid for economic development and for improving its military position. Western powers could not accommodate Somalia's military development. However, the gap was filled by the Soviet Union which willingly provided military equipment, advice, and training.[234]

TABLE 3: SOMALI GOVERNMENT EXPENDITURE (1975-81)

Item	1975	1976	1977	1978	1979	1980	1981
General Public services	33.9	31.7	32.4	35.1	31.8	31.8	32.0
Defence	25.6	25.5	25.9	37.1	39.6	41.6	43.0

---

233   Issa-Salwe, 1996: 70-5.
234   Markakis, 1990: xxiii.

Social Services	22.5	24.7	25.8	16.7	18.2	16.5	15.0
Economic Services	17.9	18.1	13.0	11.0	10.5	10.0	10.0

Source: Samatar, 1988: 101

Somalia's political aims took the toll on its economy as heavy military investment reached 3.4 per cent of the GNP. For example, the cost of arms imports in 1971-5 equalled to 43 per cent of the total non-military budget.[235] In early 1964 the average military expenditure as a percentage of GNP in Africa was 2.4. Compared to the 1976 health and education government expenses, the military expenditure, which was 6.5 percent, held more allocation than the two combined (see table 3 & 4). The following year the military expense doubled at 13.8 percent.

The era of the Somali military build-up started in this period, and was later to intensify with the involvement of superpower rivalry in the Horn. For example, in the mid 1970s Somalia possessed one of the best-equipped armed forces in sub-Saharan Africa. It was estimated that its forces reached well over 50,000. It also had more than 600 tanks and armoured personnel carriers, and over 100 modern fighter planes.[236]

The resources and energy needed for national development had been channelled into securing the liberation of what the Somali Republic termed as Somali territory 'still under

---

235 *Ibid.*, 223.
236 Makindi, 1993: 45.

colonial rule'. This policy was creating more enemies than friends. It also resulted in heightening insecurity in the Horn of Africa, and making enemies of its neighbours, Ethiopia and Kenya, and many other potential allies. Somalia was seen as in a state of war.

THE WITHDRAWAL OF THE SUPERPOWERS FROM THE HORN

In the wake of the end of the Cold War which followed the collapse of communism in the late 1980s, the Horn of Africa clients were left abandoned. From this period the Ethiopian and Somali problems mushroomed out of proportion.

The countries of the Horn were susceptible to patronage and exploitation by outside powers. As the competition of the superpowers within the region diminished with the end of the Cold War, the economic assistance injected into the region ceased. Military regimes like those of Ethiopia and Somalia were susceptible to any alteration to the external assistance which was their lifeline during the Cold War. To undermine its rival states' internal stability, both Somalia and Ethiopia had assisted the other's dissident groups. These operations were regarded by both superpowers as an "extension of the Cold War rather than as part of the old-age rivalries in the Horn".[237] Somalia had backed the Western Somali Liberation Front (WSLF), Eritrean People's Liberation Front (EPLE), Eritean Liberation Front (ELF) and Somali Abbo Liberation

---

237 Hirsch et al, 1995: 7.

Front (SALF an Oromo liberation movement). The Arab League members like Saudi Arabia also financially supported the Eritrean groups. Ethiopia in turn helped to set-up between late 1978 and early 1980 the Somali Salvation Democratic Front (SSDF), previously the Somali Salvation Front (SSF), and the Somali National Movement (SNM).

On 6 April, 1988, in Djibouti, Barre and Mengistu signed an agreement that included the end by both parties of any support for the opposition of the other.[238] Their regimes could not survive, however, beyond their agreement, as they fell victim to the global political change and the end of the Cold War. The worst hit was Somalia. During this period, evidence of Barre's violation of human rights compelled the United States to cut the economic and military assistance which it had provided Somalia from 1980s.[239] The European Community also suspended aid in 1989. Although both the United States and the European Community tied the resumption of aid with the introduction of *political* and economic **reform,** they **made** little effort towards political mediation, as the imminent crisis had engulfed Somalia in the 1990s.

---

238   Issa-Salwe, 1996: 103.
239   Makinda, 1993:56.

TABLE 4: PERCENTAGE OF GDP ALLOCATED FOR MILITARY, HEALTH, EDUCATION AND RESPECTIVE RATION (1969-78)

Year	Percentage of GDP			Radio per thousand		
	Military	Health	Educat	Armed force	Physicians	Teacher
1969	5.1	1.9	1.7	6.7	0	.7
1970	5.9	1.8	1.8	7.1	0	.7
1971	5.7	1.5	1.7	6.9	.1	.7
1972	6.2	1.8	2.4	8.6	-	1.0
1973	6.3	-	2.6	8.3	.1	1.3
1974	7.5	2.0	3.5	9.7	.1	1.3
1975	6.6	1.9	4.2	9.4	-	1.6
1976	6.5	1.8	4.6	9.7	.1	2.5
1967	7.3	2.2	5.4	16.1	-	3.0
1978	13.8	2.0	5.7	16.0	.2	-

Source: Samatar, 1988:114

THE UNRESOLVED BOUNDARY PROBLEMS

The most serious problem Somalia has faced since 1960s has been the undefined boundary with Ethiopia. On

15 December 1949, this issue came before the General Assembly and the Trusteeship Council. Following two visits to the Trust Territory in 1951 and 1954, the United Nations Visiting Mission to Italian Somaliland, reported (See Chapter-V) the growing concern over the issue of the frontier situation. A report which the mission compiled in 1951 read,

"It would be unfortunate if, in addition to the many serious problems which will unavoidably exist as the trusteeship arranged likewise inherits an unresolved boundary question".[240]

The prediction of the commission came true in the post-independence period. By the time Somalia gained its independence, the matter was still unresolved. This made Somalia concentrate its effort on the aim of putting all Somalis under a single state.

From 1974 Somalia undertook a vast international campaign to denounce what it dubbed as "the colonial" behaviour of Ethiopia towards the Somalis in Western Somaliland. Following the Ethiopian internal crisis, in early 1977 the Western Somaliland Liberation Front (WSLF) intensified its campaign. With the help of Somali regular forces, in July, WSLF launched a massive offensive and liberated nearly all the Somali-inhabited Western Somaliland within a short time by capturing main towns. However, the conflict soon assumed an international dimension when Ethiopia appealed to the Soviet Union for military assistance. The Soviet Union had decided to help Ethiopia repulse the Somali attack.

However, the defeat did not mean for Somalia the end of conflict. On the contrary, the conflict "reverted to small scale guerrilla activity" on the front and inside the Western Somaliland.[241] Economically, socially, politically and

---

240 Castagno, 1959: 387
241 Markakis, 1990: 20.

ecologically the war had profound consequences for Somalia. A wave of refugees, estimated to be more than a million, entered Somalia because of the war as well as fear of Ethiopian retaliation. To cope with the new situation, Somalia had to rely on humanitarian aid. These surges of refugees were accompanied by a flood of modern weapons from the war front into the country: a wave that was to transform Somalia.[242] On the other hand, thousands of pastoral Somalis fled from Western Somaliland with their animal stock into Somalia, creating over-grazing in many areas. The result was disastrous ecologically and produced conditions never experienced before in the country.

The Ethiopian-Somali War, also known as the Ogaden War, had led to an internal crisis as the defeat generated dissatisfaction and despondency within the army when on 9 April, 1978, a coup, led by Colonel Mahamed Sheikh Osman "Irro", was attempted and rebel troops took control of the capital. Nevertheless, the coup proved to be ill-planned and abortive. By mid-morning troops loyal to General Siyad Barre had contained the situation and rounded up some of the ringleaders in an operation which led to the death of 28 people. However, the mastermind of the coup, Colonel Abdullahi Yuusuf Ahmed, fled to Nairobi with six other associates. On 13 September 1978, Colonel Mahamed Sheikh Osman "Irro" and sixteen other officers were condemned to death by the National Security Court and they were executed on 26 October

---

242   Lewis, 30 August

1978 — 34 people were imprisoned for 10 to 20 year terms.²⁴³ The failed coup attempt was exploited by General Barre to divert attention from the country's misery resulting from his failed policies and, in order to avoid any future attempt on his regime, he took the opportunity to reconstruct the military using his inner group, thereby alienating other groups.

In response to the coup, harsh reprisals were carried out upon the accused men's kin, the Majerten. Because of this retribution, the first armed opposition movement, the Somali Salvation Front (SSF) was formed on 8 February, 1979, by Colonel Abdullahi Yuusuf Ahmed, the failed coup leader. The era of challenges to the rule of General Barre began in this period. In the next few years more opposition movements, some antagonistic to one another, were formed either in Ethiopia or in the neighbouring countries.

THE SOMALI-ETHIOPIAN PEACE AGREEMENT

While General Siyad Barre was fighting his war, Lieutenant Colonel Mengistu Haile Mariam of Ethiopia was destabilised by the conflicts in Eritrea and in Western Somaliland. In 1984 Mengistu failed in a much publicised campaign called the Red Star, which was to wipe out the Eritrean Liberation Front (ELF) and the Eritrean People's Liberation Front (EPLP) which had taken control of Karen, an important and strategic position in Eritrea. He wanted desperately to

---

243 Issa-Salwe, 1996: 92-3.

transfer the Eastern Army, which guarded the front with Somalia, to Eritrea.

Using the two Somali towns of Balan Balle and Geeldogob which had been controlled by the SSDF, with the help of the Ethiopian army since June 1982, as a bargaining counter, in October 1985, Goshe Walde, the Ethiopian Foreign Minister, officially declared these two towns part of Ethiopia. And in reaction, Colonel Abdullahi Yuusuf Ahmed, the SSDF chairman, countered furiously against the minister's assertion. SSDF found itself in the Ethiopian way at the wrong time. To clear its way, the Ethiopian authority was set to eliminate SSDF; it ordered Abdullahi Yuusuf's elimination and subsequently killed five of his bodyguards in Dire Dawa.

Both tottering in the face of internal dissent, General Siyad Barre and Lieutenant Colonel Mengistu Haile Mariam needed hostilities between the two countries to cease and the policy of helping each other's dissident groups to be stopped. With a view to easing their respective anxiety, they first met in Djibouti at the Inter-Governmental Authority for Drought and Development (IGADD) in January 1986 under the auspices of President Hassan Guled Abtidon of Djibouti, but without concluding an agreement. The difference over how to tackle border issue derailed it. Again they met on 6 April, 1988, and this time they signed an agreement that included the end by both parties of any support for the opposition of the other.

The Price of Peace

To get its share from the agreement, Haile Mariam immediately ordered the closure of SSDF and SNM radio, Radio Halgan (previously Radio Kulmis). Then he rounded up the remaining SSDF leaders and their heavy weapons, some of which had been obtained from Libya.

On the Somali part, Siyad Barre soon withdrew support from the Western Somali Liberation Front (WSLF), the Eritrean People's Liberation Front (EPLF), Eritrean Liberation Front (ELF) and Somali Abbo Liberation Front (SALF).

For Ethiopia, the peace agreement turned beneficial, while for Somalia it created a political vortex which threatened Barre's regime. Theoretically, it marked the beginning of the end of Barre's political establishment. One impact of the peace was the alienation of WSLF. The WSLF regarded the agreement as an abandonment of the Somali people still under "colonial rule", and specifically of the inhabitants of Western Somaliland. The Ogaden and their kin in the Absame and Geri clans, who make up most of the Western Somaliland inhabitants, gave all their heart to the Western Somaliland struggle. They saw the peace accord as back-stabbing by the regime of which they were one of the pillars.

Another plausible theory has it that the break-up began to develop during the Ogaden War. While the Somali army was pushing the Ethiopians out of the Ogaden, suspicion emerged about Ogaden officers taking advantage of the situation to assume control of the region and form their independent state. It was not a coincidence that the Somali regime nominated a non-Ogaden man, Abdirisaq Abubakar, as the Extraordinary Commissioner for the liberated area of the Ogaden.[244]

---

244 Markakis, 1990: 230.

CONCLUSIONS

Despite the fact that all borders are 'artificial', African borders, because of colonialism, are more artificial than others. They were created without considering the wishes of the local population, of local circumstances, such as ethnic distribution, of economic needs like land and water use, and of communication patterns. The European colonial powers left behind an enormous disorder of land and people. Ancient African kingdoms were wiped out and replaced with new nation-states. Some of these were the kingdoms of Ashanti and Benin (present Nigeria). African concern about the boundary-making began as early as the beginning of the twentieth century. Nkrumah warned in 1958 against the danger of the colonial "legacy of irredentism and tribalism", as we have seen.

When the majority of African states gained their independence within the inherited boundaries, they accepted what they inherited. They realised that by trying to reassess and redress boundary problems, they might be opening a Pandora's box. What led the African leaders to accept what they principally rejected? As the border of the state is its external shell the matter required a new approach for many African states. By defining themselves according to the inherited colonial boundaries, the majority of the African states found that for their own survival they had to respect the inherited colonial borders.[245] In many cases, the maintenance of *status quo* has come to be associated with the self-preservation of the state.

Few states have rejected the principle of accepting inherited boundaries. One of these was Somalia. Somalia's territorial claims, and Ethiopian, Kenyan and French (as former French Somaliland colonisers) counterclaims have created many international problems.

The historical evolution of the region which splintered the Somali nation, shaped the role of Somali state to unite its people within a Somali nation-state. However, this ambitious plan caused Somalia to challenge the principle of not accepting existing borders. Reunification of the Somali people served as a legitimisation of state principles after independence. President Adan Abdulle Osman declared in 1965 that "reunification of all Somalis is the very reason of life for our nation".[246]

---

245 Touval, 1963: 33.
246 Lyons, 1992: 7.

Many African states were vulnerable and suspicious of any challenge to the colonially defined boundaries for fear that the framework of their political entities would be swept away. Kenya and Ethiopia considered the problem of ethnic Somalis in their respective countries as just a matter of territorial integrity of the post-colonial state.

Both sides of the dispute in the Horn had their cases. While the Horn of African states feared Somalia's claims as a threat to their survival as states, for Somalia this constituted a dilemma, that of 'a nation in search of a state'.[247] Both cases were the antithesis of each other. Their approaches were irreconcilable. The ensuing conflict became one of the longest disputes in the African continent and furthermore, it made the Horn a rivalry platform amongst the superpowers.

Somalia: Losing the Battle

Since 1945 national self-determination has been the fundamental principle of the international community with a protocol which rejected secession. Although African states have accepted this general and restrictive usage, which amounts to equating the principle of self-- determination with anti-colonialism, they also buried any hope of compromise for territorial revision of the inherited colonially defined boundaries.

Great Britain, which felt responsible for double-dealing in the nineteenth century, was sympathetic to the Somali

---

247 Samatar et al, 1987: 129.

dilemma. In 1941, following British gain of all the Somali territories (with the exception of French Somaliland which remained under France), Ernest Bevin, the then British Foreign Secretary, recommended that all Somali territories be put under one political union under trusteeship. He read his proposal to the House of Commons on 4 June 1946. In his speech Bevin said,

> "in the latter part of the nineteenth century the Horn of Africa was divided between Great Britain, France and Italy. At about the time we occupied our part, the Ethiopians occupied an inland area which is the grazing ground for nearly half the nomads of British Somaliland, for six months of the year. Similarly, the nomads of Italian Somaliland must cross the existing frontiers in search of grass. In all innocence, therefore, we proposed that British Somaliland, Italian Somaliland, and the adjacent part of Ethiopia, if Ethiopia agreed, should be lumped together as a trust territory, so that the nomads should lead their frugal existence with the least possible hindrance and there might be a real chance of a decent economic life, as understood in that territory.... If the Conference does not like our proposal, we will not be dogmatic about it; we are prepared to see Italian Somaliland put under the United Nations' trusteeship".[248]

---

248 *Ibid,*. 35.

Nevertheless, if the British proposal (known as the Bevin Plan) was an attempt to remedy past injustices, the plan was bitterly opposed by the USSR as well as the other Allied powers, the USA and France, who were suspicious of the British proposal. Britain, as had been seen before, had tried to retain Western Somaliland as part of the Bevin Plan for Somali unification.[249]

The Soviet Union forged a close military alliance with Somalia, and signed a Treaty of Friendship and Co-operation in the 1970s. Nevertheless, it was never sympathetic to Somalia's claims which were anathema to their idea of multi-ethnic state. The Soviet Union was a country with a multitude of nationalities and the mere idea of giving every ethnic group or nationality, e.g. Uzbeks, Chechens, a separate state would be a dangerous precedent for the Soviets.

As a member of the Arab League, Somalia tried desperately to gain support against Ethiopia. However, the Arab League was also reluctant to back Somali desire for national unification. The reason partially lay in the relationship between the Arab countries and their respective superpower allies. Until the overthrow of Emperor Haile Selassie in 1974, Ethiopia was, in the words of former President Johnson, "a faithful ally of America for forty years".[250] Moreover, United States and its allies were against the disintegration of Ethiopia. Markakis regards the reason as Ethiopia's odd relationship with its Arab neighbours, which

---

249 Issa-Salwe, 1996: 45-6.
250 Legum et al, 1979: 12.

as a result was to spoil the Arab states' "dream of turning the Red Sea into an Arab lake".[251]

The influence of the United States dissuaded pro-US Arabs, such as Saudi Arabia, from supporting Somalia in its claim against Ethiopia. Pro-Soviet Arab states, on the other hand, were convinced by the Soviet Union not to sympathise with the Somali cause.[252] Although some Arab states gave tacit support, arms and aid to Somalia, yet no Arab state publicly supported Somalia's objectives for national unity.

Despite the sympathy which Somalia has gained from some quarters, it could not achieve its aim. During the writing of this book, it looked like the Somali case has taken a new course. This was demonstrated when, on 18 May 1991, approximately four months after Siyad Barre's regime was ousted, the North-Western Somali regions (what had constituted former British Somaliland) declared themselves an independent Somaliland Republic. This secession raised new concerns, not least whether this would now signal the end of the long road to pan-Somalism and the unity of the Somali nation. With this new development is the Somali case closed forever or is it only a question of time before the Somalis once again put the pieces together and re-launch their cause?

---

251 Markakis, 1990: 231.
252 Samatar et al, 1987: 133.

APPENDIX

APPENDIX I: THE ORGANIZATION OF AFRICAN UNITY CHARTER

We, the Heads of African States and Governments assembled in the City of Addis Ababa, Ethiopia,

Convinced that it is the inalienable right of all people to control their own destiny,

Conscious of the fact that freedom, equality, justice and dignity are essential objectives for the achievement of the legitimate aspirations of the African peoples,

Conscious of our responsibility to harness the natural and human resources of our continent for the total advancement of our peoples in all spheres of human endeavour,

Inspired by a common determination to promote understanding among our peoples and co-operation among our states in response to the aspirations of our peoples for brother-hood and solidarity, in a larger unity transcending ethnic and national differences,

Convinced that, in order to translate this determination into a dynamic force in the cause of human progress, conditions for peace and security must be established and maintained, **Determined** to safeguard and consolidate the hard-won independence as well as the sovereignty and territorial integrity of our states, and to fight against neo-colonialism in all its forms, **Dedicated** to the general progress of Africa,

Persuaded that the Charter of the United Nations and the Universal Declaration of Human Rights, to the Principles of which we reaffirm our adherence, provide a solid foundation for peaceful and positive co-operation among States,

Desirous that all African States should henceforth unite so that the welfare and well-being of their peoples can be assured, **Resolved** to reinforce the links between our states by establishing and strengthening common institutions,

Have agreed to the present Charter.

ESTABLISHMENT
Article 1

1. The High Contracting Parties do by the present

Charter establish the Organization to be known as the **ORGANIZATION OF AFRICAN UNITY.**

2. The Organization shall include the Continental African States, Madagascar and other Islands surrounding Africa.

PURPOSES
Article 2

1. The Organization shall have the following purposes:
   (a) To promote the unity and solidarity of the African States;
   (b) To co-ordinate and intensify their co-operation and efforts to achieve a better life for the peoples of Africa;
   (c) To defend their sovereigns, their territorial integrity and independence;
   (d) To eradicate all forms of colonialism from Africa; and
   (e) To promote intentional co-operation, having due regard to the Charter of the United Nations and the Universal Declaration of Human Rights.

2. To these ends, the Member States shall co-ordinate and harmonize their general policies, especially in the following fields:

   (a) Political and diplomatic co-operation;
   (b) Economic co-operation, including transport end communications;
   (c) Educational and cultural co-operation;
   (d) Health, sanitation and nutritional co-operation;
   (e) Scientific and technical co-operation; and
   (f) Co-operation for defence and security.

PRINCIPLES
Article 3

The Member States, in pursuit of the purposes stated in Article solemnly affirm and declare their adherence to the following principles:

1. The sovereign equality of all Member States.
2. Non-interference in the internal affairs of States.
3. Respect for the sovereignty and territorial integrity of each State' and for its inalienable right to independent existence.
4. Peaceful settlement of disputes by negotiation, mediation, conciliation or arbitration.
5. Unreserved condemnation, in all its forms, of politic' assassination as well as of subversive activities on the part a neighbouring States or any other States.
6. Absolute dedication to the total emancipation of the Africa: territories which are still dependent.
7. Affirmation of a policy of non-alignment with regard to all blocs.

MEMBERSHIP
Article 4

Each independent sovereign African State shall be entitled to become Member of the Organization.

RIGHTS AND DUTIES OF MEMBER SIATES
Article 5

All Member States shall enjoy equal rights and have equal duties.

Article 6

The Member States pledge themselves to observe scrupulously the principles enumerated in Article III of the present Charter.

INSTITUTIONS
Article 7

The Organization shall accomplish its purposes through the following principal institutions:

1. The Assembly of Heads of State and Government.
2. The Council of Ministers.
3. The General Secretariat.
4. The Commission of Mediation, Conciliation and Arbitration.

THE ASSEMBLY OF HEADS OF STATE AND GOVERNMENT
Article 8

The Assembly of Heads of State and Government shall be the supreme organ of the Organization. It shall, subject to the provisions of this Charter, discuss matters of common concern to Africa with a view to co-ordinating and harmonizing the general policy of the Organization. It may in addition review the structure, functions and acts of all the organs and any specialized agencies which may be created in accordance with the present Charter.

Article 9

The Assembly shall be composed of the Heads of State and Government or their duly accredited representatives and it shall meet at least once a year. At the request of any Member State and on approval by a two-thirds majority of the Member States, the Assembly shall meet in extraordinary session.

Article 10

1. Each Member State shall have one vote.
2. All resolutions shall be determined by a two-thirds majority of the Members of the Organization.
3. Questions of procedure shall require a simple majority. Whether or not a question is one of procedure shall be determined by a simple majority of all Member States of the Organization.
4. Two-thirds of the total membership of the Organization shall form a quorum at any meeting of the Assembly.

Article 11

The Assembly shall have the power to determine its own rule procedure.

THE COUNCIL OF MINISTERS
Article 12

1. The Council of Ministers shall consist of Foreign Ministers or other Ministers as are designated by the Governments of Member States.
2. The Council of Ministers shall meet at least twice a year. When requested by any Member State and approved by two- thirds of all Member States, it shall meet in extraordinary session.

Article 13

1. The Council of Ministers shall be responsible to the Assembly of Heads of State and Government. It shall be entrusted with the responsible of preparing conferences of the Assembly.
2. It shall take cognisance of any matter referred to it by the Assembly. It shall be entrusted with the implementation of the decision of the Assembly of Heads of State and Government. It shall co-ordinate inter-African co-operation in accordance with the instructions of the Assembly conformity with Article II (2) of the present Charter.

Article 14

1. Each Member State shall have one vote.
2. All resolutions shall be determined by a simple majority members of the Council of Ministers.
3. Two-thirds of the total membership of the Council of

Ministers shall form a quorum for any meeting of the Council.

Article 5

The Council shall have the power to determine its own rules of procedure.

GENERAL SECRETARIAT
Article 16

There shall be a Secretary-General of the Organization, who shall be appointed by the Assembly of Heads of State and Government. The Secretary-General shall direct the affairs of the Secretariat.

Article 17

There shall be one or more Assistant Secretaries-General of the Organization who shall be appointed by the Assembly of Heads of state and Government.

Article 18

The functions and conditions of service of the Secretary-General, of the Assistant Secretaries- General and other employees of the Secretariat shall be governed by the provisions of this Charter and the regulations approved by the Assembly of Heads of state and Government.

1. In the performance of their duties the Secretary-General

and the staff shall not seek or receive instructions from any government or from any other authority external to the Organization. They shall refrain from any action which might reflect on their position as international officials responsible only to the Organization.
2. Each member of the Organization undertakes to respect the exclusive character of the responsibilities of the Secretary-General and the staff and not to seek to influence them in the discharge of their responsibilities.

COMMISSION OF MEDIATION, CONCILIATION AND ARBITRATION
Article 19

Member States pledge to settle all disputes among themselves by peaceful means and, to this end decide to establish a Commission of Mediation, Conciliation and Arbitration, the composition of which and condition of service shall be defined by a separate Protocol to be approved by the Assembly of Heads of State and Government. Said Protocol shall be regarded as forming an integral part of the present Charter.

SPECIALIZED COMMISSION
Article 20

The Assembly shall establish such Specialized Commissions as it me, deem necessary, including the following:

1. Economic and Social Commission.

2. Educational, Scientific, Cultural and Health Commission.
3. Defence Commission.

Article 21

Each Specialized Commission referred to in Article XX shall composed of the Ministers concerned or other Ministers or Plenipotentiaries designated by the Governments of the Member States.

Article 22

The functions of the Specialized Commissions shall be carried out In accordance with the provisions of the present Charter and of the regulations approved by the Council of Ministers.

THE BUDGET
Article 23

The budget of the Organization prepared by the Secretary-General shall be approved by the Council of Ministers. The budget shall be provided by contribution from Member States in accordance with the scale of assessment of the United Nations; provided, however, that no Member State shall be assessed an amount exceeding twenty percent of the yearly regular budget of the Organization. The Member States agree to pay their respective contributions regularly.

SIGNATURE AND RATIFICATION OF CHARTER
Article 24

1. This Charter shall be open for signature to all independent sovereign African States and shall be ratified by the signatory States in accordance with their respective constitutional processes.
2. The original instrument, done, if possible in African languages, in English and French, all texts being equally authentic, shall be deposited with the Government of Ethiopia which shall transmit certified copies thereof to all independent sovereign African States.
3. Instruments of ratification shall be deposited with the Government of Ethiopia, which shall notify all signatories of each such deposit.

ENTRY INTO FORCE
Article 25

This Charter shall enter into force immediately upon receipt by the Government of Ethiopia of the instruments of ratification from two-thirds of the signatory States.

REGISTRATION OF CHARTER
Article 26

This Charter shall, after due ratification, be registered with the Secretariat of the United Nations through the Government of Ethiopia in conformity with Article 102 of the Charter of the United Nations.

INTERPRETATION OF THE CHARTER
Article 27

Any question which may arise concerning the interpretation of this Charter shall be decided by a vote of two-thirds of the Assembly of Heads of State and Government of the Organization.

ADHESION AND ACCESSIQN
Article 28

1. Any independent sovereign African State may at any time notify the Secretary-General of-its intention to adhere or accede to this Charter.
2. The Secretary-General shall, on receipt of such notification, communicate a copy of it to all the Member States. Admission shall be decided by a simple majority of the Member States. The decision of each Member State shall be transmitted to the Secretary-General, who shall, upon receipt of the required number of votes, communicate the decision to the State concerned.

MISCELLANEOUS
Article 29

The working languages of the Organization and all its institutions shall be, If possible African languages, English and French, Arabic and Portuguese.

Article 30

The Secretary-General may accept, on behalf of the Organization, gifts, bequests and other donations made to the Organization, provided that this is approved by the Council of Ministers.

Article 31

The Council of Ministers shall decide on the privileges and immunities to be accorded to the personnel of the Secretariat in the respective territories of the Member States.

CESSATION OF MEMBERSHIP
Article 32

Any State which desires to renounce its membership shall forward a written notification to the Secretary-General. At the end of one year from the date of such notification, if not withdrawn, the Charter shall cease to apply with respect to the renouncing State, which shall thereby cease to belong to the Organization.

AMENDMENT OF THE CHARTER
Article 33

This Charter may be amended or revised if any Member State makes a written request to the Secretary-General to that effect; provided, however, that the proposed amendment is not submitted to the Assembly for consideration until all the Member States have been duly notified of it and a period of one year has elapsed. Such an amendment shall not be effective unless approved by at least two-thirds of all the Member States.

IN FAITH WHEREOF,
We, the Heads of African State
Governments have signed this Charter.
Done in the City of Addis Ababa, Ethiopia,
25th day of May, 1963

APPENDIX II: PROTOCOL OF THE COMMISSION OF MEDIATION, CONCILIATION AND ARBITRATION

(Extracts)

Part 1: ESTABLISHMENT AND ORGANIZATION
Article 1

The Commission of Mediation, Conciliation and Arbitration established by Article 19 of the Charter of the Organization of African Unity shall be governed by the provisions of the present Protocol.

Article 2

1. The Commission shall consist of twenty-one members elected by the Assembly of Heads of State and Government.
2. No two members shall be nationals of the same State.
3. The Members of the Commission shall be persons with recognized professional qualifications.

4. Each Member State of the Organization of African Unity shall be entitled to nominate two candidates.

Article 3

1. Members of the Commission shall be elected for a term of five years and shall be eligible for re-election.
2. Members of the Commission whose terms of office have expired shall remain in office until the election of a new Commission.
3. Notwithstanding the expiry of their terms of office, Members shall complete any proceedings in which they are already engaged.

Article 4

Members of the Commission shall not be removed from office except by decision of the Assembly of Heads of State and Government, by a two-thirds majority of the total membership, on the grounds of inability to perform the functions of their office or of proved misconduct.

Article 5

1. Whenever a vacancy occurs in the Commission, it shall be Filled in conformity with the provisions of Article 2.
2. A Member of the Commission elected to fill a vacancy shall hold office for the unexpired term of the Member he has replaced.

Article 6

1. At the close of the proceedings, the Board shall draw up a report stating either:
   (a) that the parties have come to an agreement and, if the need arises, the terms of the agreement and any recommendations for settlement made by the Board, or
   (b) that it has been impossible to effect a settlement.

2. The Report of the Board of Conciliators shall be communicated to the parties and to the President of the Commission without delay and may he published only with the consent of the parties.

Part V: ARBITRATION
Article 27

1. Where it is agreed that Arbitration should he resorted to, the Arbitral Tribunal shall be established in the following manner:
   (a) each party shall designate one arbitrator from among the Members of the Commission having legal qualifications;
   (b) the two arbitrators thus designated shall, by common agreement, designate from among the Members of the Commission a third person who shall act as Chairman of the Tribunal;
   (c) where the two arbitrators fail to agree, within one month of their appointment, in the choice of the

person to be Chairman of the Tribunal, the Bureau shall designate the Chairman.

2. The President may, with the agreement of the parties, appoint to the Arbitral Tribunal two additional Members who need not be Members of the Commission but who shall have the same powers as the other Members of the Tribunal.

3. The arbitrators shall not be nationals of the parties, or have their domicile in the territories of the parties, or " be employed in their service, or have served as mediators or conciliators in the same dispute. They shall all be of different nationalities.

Article 28

Recourse to arbitration shall be regarded as submission in good faith to the award of the Arbitral Tribunal.

Article 29

1. The parties shall, in each case, conclude a compromise which shall specify:
    (a) the undertaking of the parties to go to arbitration, and to accept as legally binding, the decision of the Tribunal.
    (b) the subject matter of the controversy; and
    (c) the seat of the Tribunal.
2. The compromise may specify the law to he applied by the

Tribunal and the power, if the parties so agree, to adjudicate *ex aequo et bono*, the time-limit within which the award of the arbitrators shall be given, and the appointment of agents and counsel to take part in the proceedings before the Tribunal.

Article 30

In the absence of any provision in the *compris* regarding the applicable law, the Arbitral Tribunal shall decide the dispute according to treaties concluded between the parties, International Law, the Charter of the Organization of African Unity, the Charter of the United Nations and, if the parties agree, *ex aequo et bono*.

Article 31

1. Hearing shall be heard *in camera* unless the arbitrators decide otherwise.
2. The record of the proceedings signed by the arbitrators ad the Register shall alone be authoritative.
3. The arbitral award shall be in writing and shall, in respect of every point decide state the reason on which it is based.

APPENDIX III: RESOLUTION OF THE ALL AFRICAN PEOPLES CONFERENCE

(AAPC) 1958 and 1960
(source: Fitzgibbon, 1982)

1. First All African Peoples' Conference, Accra, 5-13 December 1958. Resolution on Frontiers, Boundaries and Federation: Whereas artificial barriers and frontiers drawn by imperialists to divide African people operate to the detriment of Africans and should therefore be abolished or adjusted.

Whereas frontiers which cut across Ethnic groups or divide people of the same stock are unnatural and are not conducive to peace or stability.

Whereas leaders of neighbouring countries should co-operate towards a permanent solution to such problems which accords with the best interests of the people affected and enhances the prospects of realisation of the ideal of a Pan-African Commonwealth of Free States.

Whereas the 20 February 1959 will be an important date in the history of the Cameroon, when a special Session of the United Nations General Assembly will discuss the question of unification and independence of the territory.

Be it resolved and it is hereby resolved by the All African Peoples' Conference that the Conference:

(a) Denounces artificial frontiers drawn by imperialist Powers to divide the peoples of Africa, particularly those which cut across ethnic groups and divide people of the same stock;

(b) Calls for the abolition or adjustment of such frontiers at an early date to this problem founded upon the true wishes of the people;

(c) Calls upon the Independent States of Africa to support a permanent solution;

(d) Notes with satisfaction that a special Session of the United

(e) ,Nations General Assembly will discuss the question of unification and independence of all the Cameroon on 20 February 1959;

(f) Invites all Africans to observe that as Cameroon Day.

2. Second All African Peoples' Conference, Tunis 25-30 January 1960, Resolution on Somaliland

3. 3. The Conference, after a careful survey of the situation in Somaliland artificially divided:

(a) Denounces the colonial repression which is dealt with in this country

(b) Hails and supports the struggle of the people of Somaliland for independence and unity in order to give birth to a bigger Somaliland;

(c) Requests the immediate liberation of detained patriots.

Appendix IV (a): Treaties between Britain and Somali Tribes, 1884-85

We, the undersigned Elders of [clan inserted here], are desirous of entering into an agreement with the British Government for the maintenance of our independence, the preservation of order and other good and sufficient reasons.

Now it is hereby agreed and covenanted as follows:—

Article I.

The [clan inserted here] do hereby declare that they are pledged and bound never to cede, sell, mortgage or otherwise give for occupation, save to the British Government, any portion of the territory presently inhabited by them or being under their control. *Article II*

All vessels under the British flag shall have free permission to trade at all ports and places within the territories of the [clan inserted here].

Article III

All British subjects, residing in, or visiting, the territories of the [clan inserted here], shall enjoy perfect safety and protection and shall be entitled to travel all over the said limits under the safe conduct of the Elders of the [clan].

Article IV

The traffic in slaves throughout the territories of the [clan inserted here] shall cease for ever, and the Commander of any of Her Majesty's vessels, or any other British Officer duly authorised, shall have the power of requiring the surrender of any slave and of supporting the demand by force of arms by land and sea.

Article V

The British Government shall have the power to appoint an agent or agents to reside in the territories of the [clan inserted here], and every such agent shall be treated with respect and consideration and be entitled to have for his protection such guard as the British Government deem sufficient. The above written treaty shall come into force and have effect from the date of signing this agreement.

In token of the conclusion of this lawful and honourable bond [names of elders inserted here], and [name of Assistant Political Resident inserted here] together with witnesses] and successors, and the latter on behalf of the British Government, do each and all in the presence of witnesses affix their signatures, marks, or seals at [place inserted here] on the [date inserted here].

APPENDIX IV (B): SUPPLEMENTARY GENERAL TREATY

[Between Britain and Somali clans, 1886.]
(source: Somali Republic Publication, 1962)

[Clan inserted here.]

The British Government have named and appointed Major Frederick Mercer Hunter, CSI, Political Agent for the Somali Coast, to conclude a treaty for this purpose.

The said Major Frederick Mercer Hunter and the said Elders of the Habr Gerhajis have agreed upon and concluded the following articles:—

Article I

The British Government, in compliance with the wish of the undersigned Elders of [clan inserted here] hereby undertake to extend to them and to the territories under their authority and jurisdiction the gracious favour and protection of Her Majesty the Queen Empress.

Article II

The said Elders of [clan inserted here] agree and promise to refrain from entering into any correspondence, agreement or treaty with any foreign nation, or power, except with the knowledge and sanction of Her Majesty's Government

Article III

This treaty shall come into operation upon the first day of February one thousand eight hundred and eighty six.

[The names of Elders inserted here.]
(Signed) F. M. HUNTER, Major,
Political Agent, Somali Coast.

APPENDIX V: AGREEMENT BETWEEN BRITAIN AND THE OGADEN

(1st September, 1896)
(source: Somali Republic, 1962)

I, Ahmed Murgan, the Chief of the Ogaden tribe, do hereby place myself, my people, and country, with its dependencies, under the protection of Her Britannic Majesty the Queen, and do hereby declare that I will not, nor shall my successors or any of my people, cede or alienate any portion of my territories or independence, or make any Treaties with any foreign State or person, without the previous knowledge and sanction of Her Majesty's Government.

Commercial arrangements between me and non-natives shall be subject to the approval of Her Majesty's Representative, who shall regulate all disputes, and by whose I will be guided in all my relations with non-natives.

Witness:

(Signatures in Arabic)
Before me,
J.W. Tritton
A.C.W. Jenner,
Sub-Commissioner.

APPENDIX VI: TREATY OF PROTECTION BETWEEN FRANCE AND THE CHIEFS OF THE ISSA SOMALIS

(source: Somali Republic Publication, 1962)

Between M. Lagarde (A.M.J.L), Governor of the Colony of Obock, acting in the name of the French Government, and the Issa Chiefs hereinafter defined:

Abdi Handel, Roble Tonke, Barre Ali, Beder Gedi, Gedi Dagah, Dirane Dedis, Roble Guled, Hassan Gedi, Gedi Roble, Muse Said, Maherame Ige, Waes Garbabud, Gedi Hersi, Geri Jibelbor, Allale Waes, Assobi Bonis, Oure Barre, Waes Guled, Buhe Dirir, who control the territory extending from Gubbet Kharak and beyond Ambaddo near Zeyla, the following Treaty has been signed:

Art. I - There shall henceforth be eternal friendship between France and the Chiefs of Issa.

Art. II - The Chiefs of the Issa hand over their territory to France that she may protect it against all foreign.

Art. III - The France Government undertakes to facilitate commerce on the coast and especially at Ambaddo.

Art. IV - The Issa Chiefs undertake to assist France at all times and to sign no Treaty nor conclude any agreement, under penalty of nullity, without the consent of the Governor of Obock.

Obock, the 26th March, 1885.
(sd) Lagarde,
Governor of the Colony
(Mark of the Issa Chiefs)

MAPS

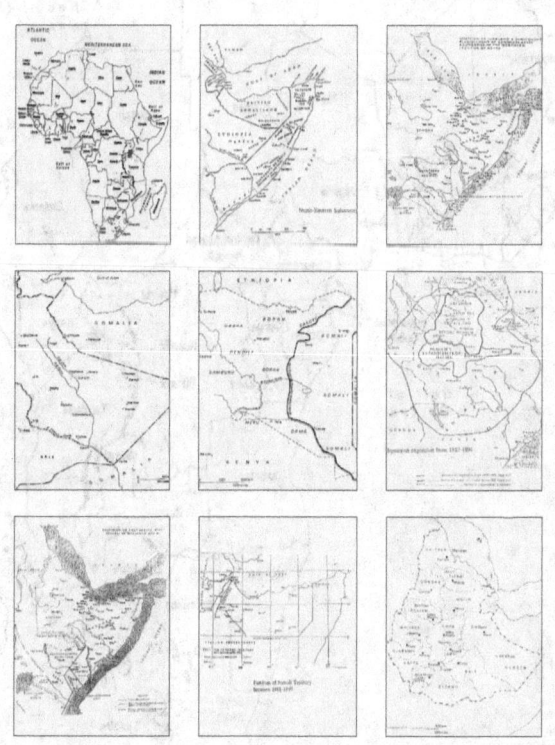

Africa

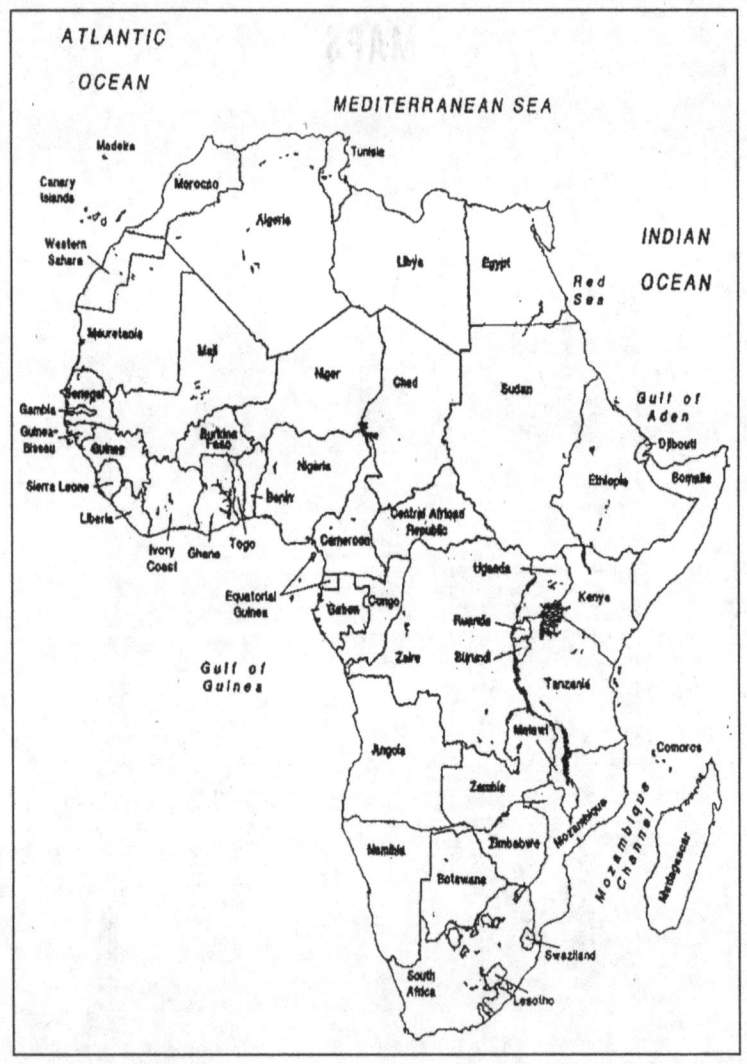

North-Eastern Sultanates

North-Eastern Sultanates

SECESSION OF JUBBALAND

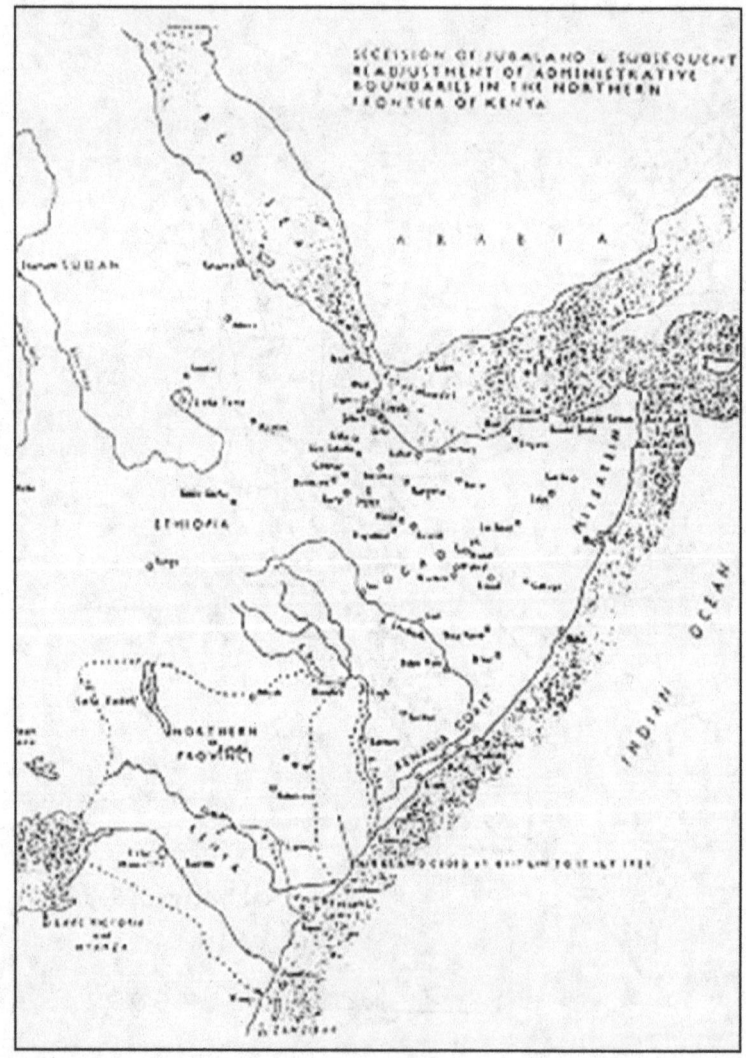

The Ogaden (Western Somaliland)

North-Eastern District Frontier (NFD)

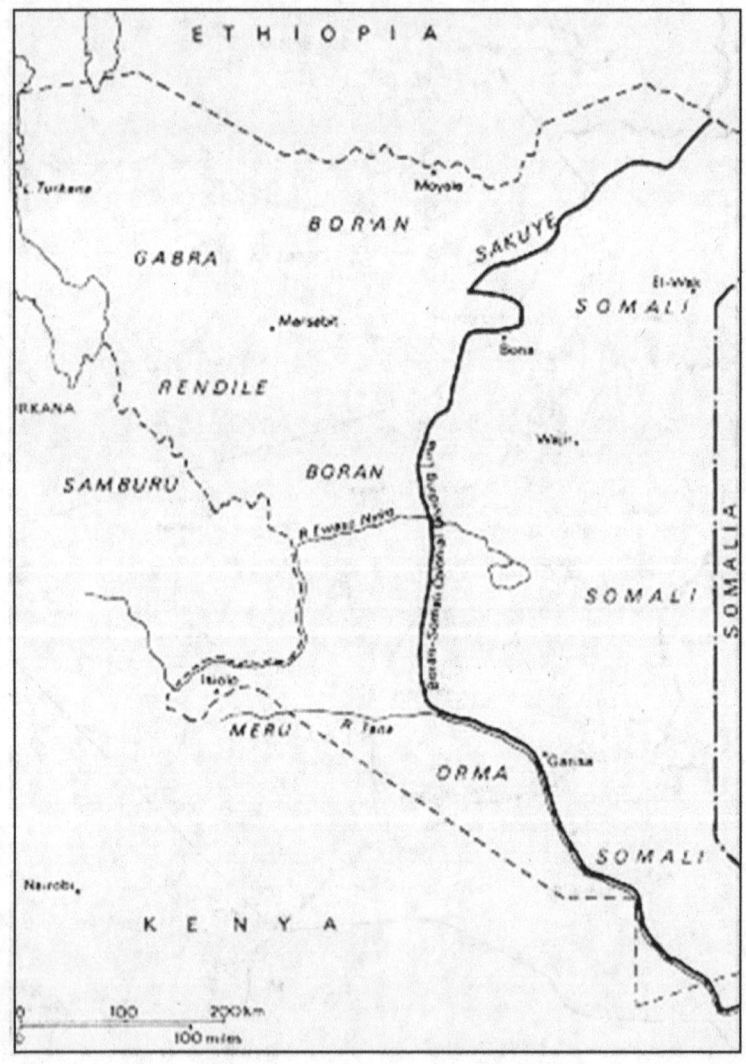

MAPS

ABYSSINIAN EXPANSION FROM 1887 TO 1891

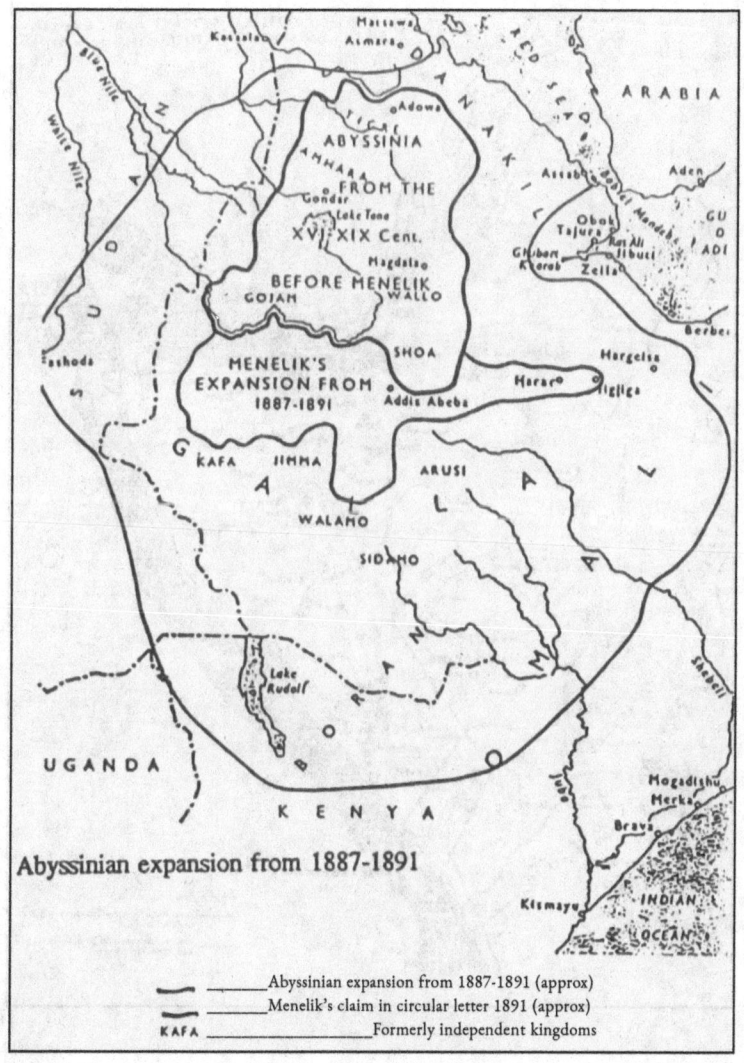

Partition of East Africa into Spheres of Influence 1890 to 1891

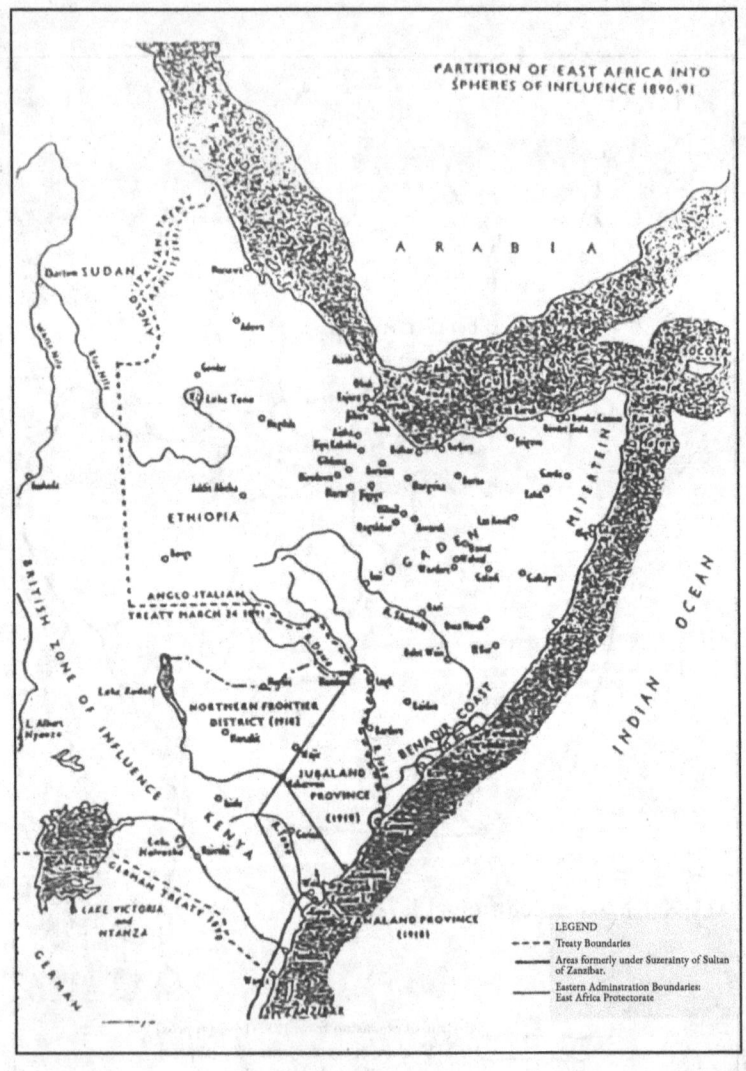

PARTITION OF SOMALI TERRITORY BETWEEN 1888-1894

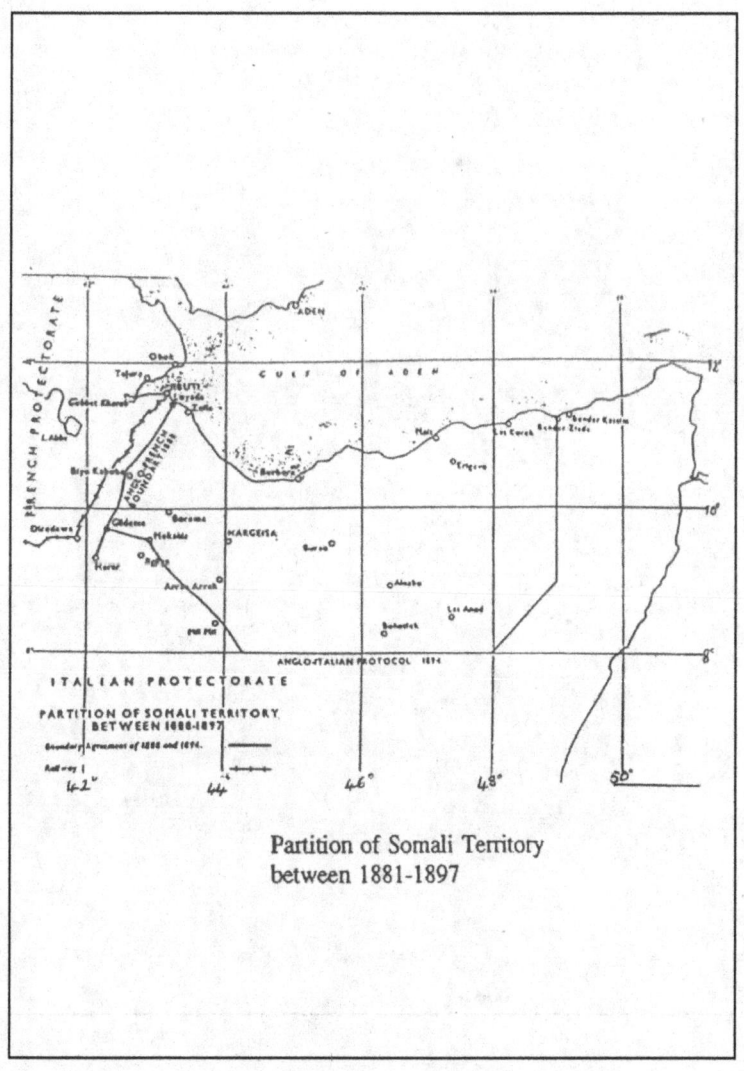

Partition of Somali Territory between 1881-1897

MODERN ETHIOPIA

BIBLIOGRAPHY

Ben-Israel, Hevda; "Irredentism: Nationalism Reexamined" in Naomi Ghazan, (ed); *Irredentism and International Politics;* (Boulder: Lynne Rienner Publishers, Inc., 1991).

Bhardwaj, Raman G.; *The Dilemma of the Horn of Africa,* (New Delhi: Sterling Publishers Pvt Ltd, 1979).

Brzezinski, Zbigniew, (ed.); *Africa and the Communist World,* (Stanford, California: Stanford University Press, 1964).

--------; *Power and Principle: Memoirs of the National Security Adviser, 1977-1981,* (London: Weidenfeld and Nicolson, 1983).

Calvocoressi, Peter; *World Politics Since 1945,* 6th edn., (London: Longman, 1991).

Castagno, A.A. Jr.; "Somalia", in *International Conciliation,*

New York, March 1959.

Dallin, Alexander; "The Soviet Union: Political Activity", in *Africa and the Communist World,* by Zbigniew Brzezinski, (ed.), (Stanford, California: Stanford University Press, 1964).

Del Boca, Angelo; *Gli Italiani in Africa Orientale: Nostalgia delle Colonie,* (Roma: Editori Laterza, 1984), Vol IV.

Farah, Mohammed I.; *From Ethnic Response to Clan Identity: A Study of State Penetration among the Somali Nomadic Pastoral Society of Northeastern Kenya,* (Doctoral Dissertation at Uppsala University, Uppsala 1993).

Fitzgibbon, Louis; *The Betrayal of the Somalis,* (London: Rex Collings Ltd., 1982).

Ghazan, Naomi; "Approaches to the Study of Irredentism" in Naomi Ghazan, (ed); *Irredentism and International Politics;* (Boulder: Lynne Rienner Publishers, Inc., 1991).
Gobban, Alfred; *National Self-determination,* (London Oxford

University Press 1945).

Hess, Robert L., *Italian Colonialism in Somalia,* (Chicago: The University of Chicago Press, 1966).

Hirsch, John L. And Rober B. Oakley, *Somalia and Operation Restore Hope: Reflections on Peacemaking and Peacemaking, (Washington:* United States Institute of Peace, 1995).

Issa-Salwe, Abdisalam M.; *The Collapse of the Somali State. The Impact of the Colonial Legacy*, New Edn. (London: Haan Publishers, 1996).

Jones, A H M; and Monroe, Elizabeth; *A History of Abyssinia,(Oxford:* Oxford University Press, 1937).

Legum, Colin; and Bill Lee, *The Horn of Africa in Continuing Crisis*, (New York: Africana Publishing Company, 1979).

Lewis, I M; *A Modern History of Somalia: Nation and State in the Horn of Africa* (London: Longman, 1980).

--------; (ed); *Nationalism & Self Determination in the Horn of Africa*, (London: Ithaca Press London, 1983)

--------; *A Pastoral Democracy*, (London: Oxford University Press, 1961).

--------; *Peoples of the Horn of Africa: Somali, Afar and Saho*, 2nd edn. (London: Haan Associates for the International African Institute, 1994).

--------; "The Ogaden and the Fragility of Somali Segmentary Nationalism", *Horn of Africa*, Vol. XIII, No.1 &2, Jan-March April-Jun 1990.

--------; "In the Land of the Living Dead", The Sunday Times, 30 August

Lowenthal, Richard; "China" in *Africa and the Communist World*, ed. by Brzezinski, Zbigniew, (Stanford, California: Stanford University Press, 1964).

Lyons, Terrence, "Crises on Multiples Levels: Somalia and the Horn of Africa, in *The Somali Challenge: Peace, Resources and Reconstruction, Geneva, 10-14 July 1992.*

Makinda, Samuel; *Seeking Peace From Chaos: Humanitarian Intervention in Somalia,* (Boulder, Colorado: Lynne Rienner Publishers, 1993).

Markakis, John; *National and Class Conflict in the Horn of Africa,* (London: Zed Books, 1990)

Mayall, James, "Self-Deterrnination and the OAU" in I. M. Lewis (ed.); *Nationalism & Self Determination in the Horn of Africa,* (London: Ithaca Press London, 1983).

Mazrui, Ali; and Tidy, Michael; *Nationalism and New States of Africa,* (Nairobi: Heinemann, 1984).

Miller, David; ed., *Blackwell Encyclopaedia of Political Thought,* (Oxford: Basil Blackwell Ltd., 1987).

Naldi, Gino J; *The Organization of African Unity: An Analysis of its Role,* (London: Mansel Publishing Limited, 1989)

Neuberger, Benyarnin; "Irredentism and Politics in Africa" in Naomi Ghazan, (ed), *Irredentism and International Politics,* (Boulder: Lynne Rienner Publishers, Inc., 1991).

Omar, Mohamed Osman; *The Road to Zero: Somalia's Self-Destruction,* (London: Haan Associates, 1992).

Perham, Margery; *The Government of Ethiopia,* (Evanston, Illinois: North Western University Press, 1969).

Porter, Bruce D., *The USSR in Third World Conflicts: Soviet Arms and Diplomacy in Local War 1945-1980*, (Cambridge: Cambridge University Press, 1984).

Reisman W. Michael, "Somali Self-determination in the Horn: Legal Perspectives and Implications for Social and Political Engineering" in I. M. Lewis (ed); *Nationalism & Self Determination in the Horn of Africa*, (London: Ithaca Press London, 1983).

Rinehart, Robert; "Historical Setting" in *Somalia: A Country Study*, ed. by Harold D. Nelson, (Washington: Arnerican University, 1982).

Samatar, Said S. Laitin, David D.; *Somalia: Nation in Search of a State* (Bouler, Colorado: Westview Press, 1987).

"Somali Constitution", Somali Government Publication, 1991, Muqdisho, Somalia.

Somali Republic, Government of The; *The Somali Peninsula. A New Light on Imperial Motives*, Information Service, Mogadisho, 1962.

Tordoff, William; *Government and Politics in Africa*, (London: McMillan Education Ltd., 1990).

Touval, Saadia; *Somali Nationalism: International Politics and the Drive for Unity in the Horn of Africa*, (Cambridge: Harvard University Press, 1963).

--------; *The Boundary Politics of Independent Africa*, (Cambridge, Massachusetts: Harvard University Press, 1972).

Trimingham, Spencer J.; *Islam in Ethiopia*, (Oxford: the Clarendon Press, 1952).

INDEX

A. H. Hardinge, 65
Aadan Abdulle, i, 85, 98, 116, 117, 119, 180
AAPC, vi, 19, 20, 42, 203
Abdirisaaq Abubakar, 178
Abdirisaaq Haaji Husein, 116, 119
Abdullaahi Issa, 98
Abdullaahi Yuusuf, 174, 175
Absame, 177
Abyssinia, 66, 71, 87, 111, 222
Accra, 17, 19, 48, 124, 203
Adal, 111
Addis Ababa, x, 35, 36, 38, 84, 90, 98, 105, 121, 124, 147
Aden, 63, 138, 139, 151, 154
Adowa, 66, 94
Afar, 110, 115, 222
Afghanistan, 60, 156
AFRICA, i, vi, viii, ix, 1, 2, 3, 5, 6, 8, 9, 10, 11, 13, 18, 19, 20, 21, 23, 24, 25, 26, 27, 29, 30, 33, 34, 35, 36, 40, 41, 42, 44, 45, 52, 53, 54, 55, 56, 57, 58, 59, 61, 62, 63, 64, 66, 67, 68, 77, 82, 85, 87, 88, 89, 94, 101, 102, 111, 112, 127, 129, 137, 138, 140, 141, 142, 144, 149, 150, 151, 152, 155, 160, 162, 168, 169, 182, 203, 204, 221, 222, 223, 224, 225
Alexander Dallin, 56
Algeria, 20, 23, 27, 85, 100
Algiers, 134
All African People's Conference, 19
Allied Council of Foreign Ministers, 72
Almorabid Empire, 27
Aman Andom, 145
American Colonisation Society for the Establishment of Free Men of Colour, 33

Andrew Young, 162 Anglo-
Ethiopian Boundary
Commission, 28
Anglo-German Agreement, 64
AngloSomali Treaties of
Protection, 97
Anglo-Somali Treaties of
Protection, 67
Angola, vi, 61, 62, 149, 154
Angolan war, 60
Anwar Sadat, 141
Aouzou Strip, 26
Apartheid, 41
Arab, 4, 9, 13, 25, 27, 140, 141, 144, 147, 148, 153, 156, 163, 170, 183, 184 Arab League, 183
Armis, 142
Arusha, 109, 117, 119, 121, 123, 128
Arusha Memorandum, 119
Ashanti, 179
Asia, 6, 54, 82, 137
Assab, 150, 164
Awash, x, 90
Awdal, 111
Bab-el-Mandeb, 111, 116, 138, 140, 141, 163
Bakongo, 25
Balan Balle, 175
Banjul Charter, 46
Barre, 130, 147, 170, 174, 175, 177, 208
Bathurst, 13
Beijing, 53
Belgium, 13, 149
Benaadir, 69, 96
Benin, 26, 179
Ben-Israel, 24, 221
Berbera, 142, 143, 156, 162

Berlin, 14, 70
Berlin Conference, 14, 70
Bevin, 72, 182, 183
Bhardwaj, 15, 68, 77, 111, 138, 141, 143, 148, 153, 158, 163
Biafra, 134
Bolshevik, 54
Boqor Osmaan, 69, 70
Borku-Enmedi Tibesti, 26
Botswana, 25
Brazzaville bloc, 20, 59
Brett, 14
Brezhnev, 62
Britain, xi, 13, 14, 28, 52, 63, 64, 65, 66, 67, 70, 72, 73, 74, 76, 77, 82, 91, 92, 93, 97, 104, 107, 108, 109, 120, 129, 138, 139, 141, 144, 167, 181, 182, 183, 204, 206
British Colonial Secretary, 106
British East Africa Company, 65
British Foreign Office, 65 British Somaliland, x, 71, 72, 74, 182
Brzezinski, i, 2, 52, 53, 150, 154, 159, 160, 161, 162, 221, 223
Burkina Faso, 43
Cairo, 39, 85
Cameroon, 13, 26, 203, 204
Candole Line, 76
Cape Guardafui, 63
Carter, 2, 153, 154, 155, 156, 159, 160, 162
Casablanca bloc, 20, 59
Castro, 145
Ceuta and Metilla, 27 Chad, 26
Charter of the Organization of African Unity, 30, 199, 202

INDEX

Chechens, 183
Chewa, 25
China, 53, 65, 141, 147, 223
Christian Democrats, 73
CIAS, vi, 19, 20
Cold War, 1, 7, 8, 9, 11, 51, 52, 59, 140, 165, 169, 170
Commission of Mediation, Conciliation and Arbitration, 45, 199
Commonwealth, 107, 108, 203
Conference of Independent African States, vi, 19 Congo, 13, 20, 99
Congo Free State, 14 Congress of Berlin, 33
Cushitic, 111
Cyrenaica, 72
Danakil, 111
Danod, 75
Daraawiish, 82
Dar-es-Salaam, 99, 100, 166
Dayan, 163
de Gaulle, 113
Dervish, 82
Dhagahbuur, 71, 146
Diego Garcia, 144, 155
Dire Dawa, 146, 172, 176
Djibouti, 4, 66, 74, 81, 83, 90, 110, 112, 113, 115, 116, 119, 137, 138, 170, 176
Duncan Sandys, 107
EACSO, vi, 88
East African Association, 88 East African Common Services Organisation, 88
EDU, 144
Egypt, 4, 19, 63, 64, 138, 139, 141, 152, 159

ELF, vi, 170, 175, 177
EPLF, vi, 177
EPLP, 175
EPRP, 144
Equatorial Guinea, 26
Eritrea, 71, 72, 74, 77, 78, 96, 97, 111, 112, 137, 139, 143, 150, 162, 164, 175
Eritrean Liberation Front, 175
Eritrean People's Liberation Front, vi, 170, 175, 177
Eritrean Republic, 6, 141
Ethiopia, x, xi, 1, 2, 4, 5, 7, 9, 10, 19, 23, 27, 28, 29, 30, 39, 63, 67, 70, 71, 73, 74, 75, 76, 77, 78, 81, 82, 83, 84, 85, 86, 88, 89, 90, 91, 92, 93, 94, 95, 96, 97, 98, 99, 100, 101, 102, 111, 112, 113, 114, 115, 116, 118, 120, 124, 125, 126, 127, 128, 130, 131, 137, 138, 143, 144, 145, 146, 147, 148, 150, 151, 152, 153, 154, 156, 157, 159, 161, 163, 164, 166, 169, 171, 172, 175, 177, 180, 182, 183, 184, 224
Ethiopian Democratic Union, 144
Ethiopian Empire, 89, 97
Ethiopian People's Revolutionary Party, 144
Ethiopian Revolutionary Government, 145
Europe, 6, 21, 52, 137, 158
European, viii, 7, 13, 14, 16, 17, 18, 42, 48, 63, 64, 66, 67, 70, 94, 112, 138, 141, 149, 153, 170, 179
European Community, 170

Ewe, 25, 26
Extraordinary Commissioner, 178
Fang, 26
Far East, 63
Federation of Ethiopia, 74
FeerFeer, 92
Fenando Poo, 26
Fer-fer, 92
Fitzgibbon, 88
Four Powers Commission, 72
France, 4, 14, 52, 65, 66, 67, 70, 72, 74, 110, 113, 115, 116, 119, 125, 126, 128, 138, 141, 149, 166, 182, 183, 208, 209
French Somaliland, 66, 71, 112
French Territory of the Afars and Ises, 115
Fulani, 25
Gabra, 103
Gadaduma, 28, 29, 128
Gaffar Al Nimery, 140
Geel-dogob, 175
General Act, 70
General Assembly, 32, 47, 73, 75, 114, 171, 203, 204
Geri, 177, 208
Germany, 14, 52, 64, 70
Ghana, 18, 19, 23, 26, 33, 34, 99
Godama, 29
Goday, 146
Gold Coast, 13
Goshe Walde, 175
Greater Somalia, 83
Haile Mariam, 146, 175, 176
Haile Selassie, 71, 75, 96, 112, 113, 144, 150, 164, 184
Harar, 63, 64, 66, 111
Hararghe, x, 90

Hassan Guled Abtidon, 176
Hassaniya, 26
Haud, xi, 68, 72, 74
Hausas, 26
Hawd, xi, 68, 72, 73, 74, 75, 77, 91, 93
Hobyo, 69, 70
Hobyo Sultanate, 69
Hodayo, 95
Horn, viii, ix, x, 1, 2, 5, 6, 8, 9, 10, 63, 66, 67, 68, 71, 77, 78, 94, 111, 112, 127, 129, 137, 138, 139, 140, 141, 142, 144, 146, 147, 149, 150, 151, 153, 155, 156, 158, 159, 161, 163, 165, 168, 169, 181, 182, 221, 222, 223, 224
House of Commons, 69, 182
Ibos, 26
Ibrahim Abboud, 91, 101
ICBM, 143
ICJ, vi, 32, 43, 44
Igaal, 119, 120, 121, 124
IGADD, vi, 176
Imperial Powers, 18
Indian Ocean, 63, 138, 139, 142, 143, 149
Indochina, 60
Indo-Pakistani war, 60
Ingwavuma District, 25
Inter-Continental Ballistic Missile, 143
Inter-Governmental Authority for Drought and Development, 176
International Court of Justice, vi, 32
International Covenant on Civil and Political Rights, 31

International Covenant on Economic, Social and Cultural Rights, 31
Israel, 163
Issa Somalis, 111, 115, 208
Italian Somaliland, x, 72, 182
Italo-Ethiopian Agreements, 75
Italy, 14, 52, 66, 67, 69, 70, 71, 72, 73, 75, 76, 82, 92, 141, 182
Japan, 158
Jigjiga, x, xi, 90, 146
Joint Declaration, 123
Jomo Kenyatta, 104, 116
Jubbaland, 65
KADU, vi, 88, 105
Kagnew, 143, 144
KaNgwane, 25
KANU, vi, 105
Karen, 175
Keenadiid, 69
Kenneth Kaunda, 120
Kenya, vi, 4, 5, 7, 10, 23, 27, 28, 29, 30, 71, 77, 78, 81, 83, 84, 85, 86, 88, 90, 91, 96, 99, 100, 102, 103, 104, 105, 106, 107, 108, 109, 110, 115, 116, 117, 118, 120, 121, 123, 124, 125, 126, 127, 128, 130, 131, 151, 156, 166, 169, 180, 221
Kenya African National Union, vi, 105
Kenya Constitutional Conference, 104
Kenyatta, 105, 117, 118, 124
Khartoum, 101, 124
Khedive Ismail, 63
King Leopold II, 13
Kinshasa, 121, 123, 124, 126, 129

Kismaayo, 64, 65, 142
Konainge, 117
Kwazulu, 25
Lagos, 13, 20
Laitin, 5, 86, 224
Lake Rudolf, 71
Lancaster House, 104
Lenin, 54
Lesotho, 25
Lewis, 40, 68, 95, 113
Liberia, 4, 19
Libya, 19, 26, 72, 99, 176
London, 104, 221, 222, 223, 224
Lord Acton, 24
Lord Curzon, 22
Luanda, 25
Madagascar, 65
Mahamed Haaji Ibrahim, 119, 124
Mahamed Sheikh Osmaan "Irro", 174
Mahdist Movement, 64
Majeerteen, 69, 174
Majeerteen Sultanate, 69
Mali, 26, 27, 43
Manchester, 18, 42, 48
Markakis, 74, 103, 137, 145, 167, 168, 173, 178, 184
Massawa, 111, 150, 162, 164
Mauritania, 20, 23, 26, 27, 32
Mayall, 20, 40, 41, 42
Menelik, 66, 67, 111
Monrovia, 20, 34, 35, 59, 98
Morocco, 19, 20, 23, 26, 27, 32, 39, 85, 100
Moscow, 2, 53, 55, 56, 57, 58, 59, 60, 61, 139, 147, 148, 150, 152, 153, 154, 159
Moyale, xi, 90, 103

Muqdisho, 71, 76, 124, 142, 147, 152, 153, 224
Murumbi, 117
Muslim world, 82
Mussolini, 94
Nairobi, 107, 117, 119, 174, 223
Naldi, 33, 36, 43, 223
National Congress, 17, 48
National Review, 101
NATO, 143, 156, 162
NFD, vi, 65, 84, 90, 91, 95, 96, 102, 103, 104, 105, 106, 107, 108, 109, 121, 125, 165
Ngoni, 25
Niger, 26
Nigeria, 99, 179
Nile Valley, 27
Nkrumah, 18, 19, 21, 34, 35, 179
non-aligned countries, 9
Northeastern Province, 134
North-Eastern Province, 84, 102
Northern Frontier District, vi, 65, 83, 84, 102, 104, 106, 108
Nyerere, 109, 117, 123
OAU, vi, 2, 6, 8, 9, 10, 27, 35, 36, 37, 39, 41, 45, 48, 49, 84, 85, 87, 91, 94, 95, 99, 100, 101, 102, 112, 113, 114, 119, 123, 126, 129, 131, 151, 152, 158, 161, 166
OAU Charter, 35, 151
OAU Liberation Committee, 112
Obok, 65
Ochoa, 154
Ogaadeen, x, xi, 1, 2, 60, 64, 68, 71, 75, 83, 87, 89, 91, 92, 95, 110, 112, 148, 151, 152, 153, 157, 160, 163, 173, 177

Organisation of African Unity, 6, 7, 35, 101, 105, 115
Orma, 103
Oromo, vi, 102, 170
PAFMECA, vi, 19
pan-African Freedom Movement of East and Central Africa, 19
pan-Africanism, 10, 18, 33
Paris, 134
Pax-Sovietica, 145
People's Democratic Republic of Yemen, 60, 145
Petrov, 154
Podgorny, 145
Portugal, 14, 52
Potsdam Conference, 72
Qabridaharre, 71
Qallafo, 71
R. J. Harrison Church, 3, 21
Radio Halgan, 176
Radio Kulmis, 176
Ramu, 110
Rapid Development Task Force, 156
Ras Waldo Gabriel, 111
Red Sea, 63, 65, 71, 74, 138, 139, 140, 141, 149, 150, 151, 156, 162, 163, 164, 184
Red Star, 175
Reginald Maulding, 106
Reisman, 32, 70, 97, 224
Rendille, 103
Reserved Area, xi, 68, 73, 74, 77, 93
Rio Muni, 26
River Tana, 64
Rome, 76, 108, 118
Ronald Ngala, 88, 105

Royal Charter, 65
Rupert Emerson, 8, 42
Russia, 2, 54, 61, 139, 141, 150, 158, 164
Saharan Arab Democratic Republic, 4, 27
Sahrawi, 33
Saigon, 61
Sakuye, 103
SALF, vi, 170, 177
SALT, i, vii, 2, 159, 160, 162
Samatar, 5, 37, 68, 69, 86, 90, 93, 95, 120, 131, 161, 162, 166, 167, 171, 181, 183, 184, 224
Saudi Arabia, 141, 144, 152, 153, 154, 159, 162, 170, 184
Sayid Mahamed, 82 Second Word War, 51 Second World War, 71, 96
Security Council, 99, 100, 101
Senegal, 13
Sharmaarke, 88, 105, 116, 119, 166
shifta, 96, 109, 118, 124, 127
Sierra Leone, 13
Siyaad Barre, viii, 130, 147, 162, 174, 175, 176, 177
SNM, vii, 170, 176
Somali National Assembly, 98, 104, 121, 166
Somali National Movement, vii, 170
Somali Republic, i, 5, 23, 68, 81, 83, 88, 103, 104, 106, 107, 149, 165, 168, 206, 207, 208, 224
Somali Salvation Front, vii, 170, 174

Somalia, viii, ix, x, 1, 2, 4, 5, 7, 9, 10, 11, 23, 25, 29, 30, 39, 70, 72, 75, 76, 77, 82, 83, 84, 85, 86, 87, 88, 89, 90, 91, 92, 93, 94, 96, 98, 99, 100, 101, 102, 104, 106, 108, 109, 110, 111, 112, 113, 114, 115, 116, 117, 118, 119, 120, 122, 123, 124, 125, 126, 127, 128, 129, 130, 131, 137, 140, 142, 145, 146, 147, 148, 150, 151, 152, 154, 155, 156, 161, 163, 165, 166, 167, 168, 169, 170, 171, 172, 173, 175, 177, 180, 181, 183, 184, 221, 222, 223, 224
Somali-Ethiopian dispute, 98, 140
Somaliland, x, xi, 64, 65, 66, 68, 69, 71, 72, 73, 74, 81, 82, 83, 87, 89, 90, 92, 93, 95, 97, 98, 110, 112, 113, 115, 125, 131, 145, 146, 150, 156, 165, 166, 172, 173, 175, 177, 180, 181, 182, 183, 204
Sothos, 25
South Africa, 25, 61 Southern Africa, vi
Soviet Union, 1, 2, 9, 51, 53, 54, 56, 58, 60, 61, 73, 129, 139, 140, 141, 142, 145, 146, 147, 148, 150, 151, 152, 153, 155, 161, 162, 167, 173, 183, 184, 221
SSDF, vii, 170, 175, 176
SSF, vii, 170, 174
Stalin, 54
Strategic Arms Limitation Treaty, 2

Sublime Porte, 63
Sudan, 19, 27, 63, 64, 67, 82, 137, 140, 144, 152, 156
Suez, 63, 127, 139, 140, 141, 149, 162
Sultan of Zanzibar, 64, 69
Sultan Yuusuf, 69
Swaziland, 25
Swazis, 25
Tafari Banti, 145
Tana, 65, 103
Tanganyika, 88
Tanzania, 88, 109, 117, 119, 120
the Dergue, 145, 148, 149
the Gulf, 138, 143, 162, 163
the Nile, 27, 65, 67, 137, 138
Third World, 47, 62, 224
Togo, 23, 26
Togoland, 13
Tordoff, 3, 13, 42, 85
Touval, 7, 8, 16, 21, 22, 28, 29, 30, 42, 48, 89, 98, 105, 107, 108, 113, 114, 115, 117, 121, 130, 180
Treaty of Friendship and Co-operation, 142, 147, 183
Treaty of Uccialli, 66
Trust Territory, 93, 171
Trusteeship, 75, 76, 92, 171
Trygve Lie, 76, 92
Tswanas, 25
Tunisia, 19, 26, 27, 99
Turkey, 63, 143
U Thant, 100
Uganda, 88, 120, 123
UN Charter, 32, 36, 37, 38, 45
UN Trusteeship, 93
Union Africaine et Malgache, 20
Unita, 61

United Nations, vii, 31, 49, 75, 92, 93, 109, 112, 113, 114, 115, 126, 172, 183, 202, 203
United States, 9, 33, 34, 55, 61, 62, 73, 129, 140, 142, 143, 146, 150, 152, 155, 156, 159, 160, 161, 162, 170, 184, 222
Upper Volta, 43
USSR, 54, 55, 56, 60, 72, 141, 146, 153, 183, 224
Uzbeks, 183
Vance, 155, 159, 161, 162
Vichy rule, 71
Vietnam, 61
Volta Region, 26
Wal Wal, 70
Wal-waal, 70
Warsheikh, 64
Washington, 2, 61, 62, 139, 142, 143, 152, 156, 158, 159, 160, 161, 222, 224
West, xi, 2, 8, 13, 18, 51, 53, 55, 56, 58, 61, 62, 90, 116, 138, 139, 141, 147, 150, 151, 152, 153, 158
West Africa, 13, 18
Western Sahara, 26, 27, 32
Western Somali Liberation Front, vii, 95, 146, 170, 177
Western Somaliland, x, xi, 68, 90, 146, 172, 173, 177
WSLF, vii, 95, 146, 170, 172, 177
Yao, 25
Yemen, 60, 140, 151
Yom Kippur war, 60 Yorubas, 26
Zambia, 120, 124
Zande, 25
Zeyla, 63, 66, 73, 111, 208

www.ingramcontent.com/pod-product-compliance
Lightning Source LLC
Chambersburg PA
CBHW011957090526
44590CB00023B/3758